4/2

D1201672

# Information Management Systems: Data Base Primer

**PETROCELLI/CHARTER COMPUTER SCIENCE SERIES**
edited by Ned Chapin

**Computers and Management for Business**
Douglas A. Colbert

**Management of Information Technology: Case Studies**
Elizabeth B. Adams, editor

**Reliable Software Through Composite Design**
Glenford J. Myers

**Strategic Planning of Management Information Systems**
Paul Siegel

**Top-Down Structured Programming Techniques**
Clement L. McGowan and John R. Kelly

**Operating Systems Principles**
Stanley Kurzban, Thomas S. Heines, and Anthony P. Sayers

**Hospital Computer Systems and Procedures, Vol. 1: Accounting Systems**
Raymon D. Garrett

**Flowcharts**
Ned Chapin

**Operating Systems Survey**
Anthony Sayers, editor

**Logical Design for Computers and Control**
K. N. Dodd

**Flowcharting: An Introductory Text and Workbook**
John K. Lenher

**Compiler Techniques**
Bary W. Pollack, editor

**Documentation Manual**
Julia van Duyn

**Computer Techniques in Biomedicine and Medicine**
Enoch Haga, editor

**Hospitals—A Systems Approach**
Raymon D. Garrett

**Management of EDP**
M. M. Wofsey

**Introduction to Artificial Intelligence**
Philip C. Jackson

**Software Engineering: Concepts and Techniques**
J. M. Buxton, Peter Naur, and Brian Randell, editors

# Information
# Management
# Systems

## DATA BASE PRIMER

## Vivian C. Prothro

 PETROCELLI/CHARTER    NEW YORK 1976

Randall Library UNC-W

Copyright © Mason/Charter Publishers, Inc. 1976

All rights reserved. No part of this work covered by the copyrights hereon may be reproduced or used in any form or by any means—graphic, electronic, or mechanical, including photocopying, recording, or taping, or information storage and retrieval systems—without written permission of the publisher.

Printed in the United States of America

1 2 3 4 5 6 7 8 9 10

Library of Congress Cataloging in Publication Data

Prothro, Vivian C
    Information management systems.

    Includes index.
    1. Data base management.  I. Title.
QA76.9.D3P78    001.6'442      76-44481
ISBN 0-88405-336-9

# Contents

QA76
.9
.D3
.P78

240928

**Preface    vii**

**1. The Data Base Era    1**

Operating System Extensions    4

**2. Definition of Terms    17**

EAM Equipment    17
File/Data Set    17
Application Program (A/P)    19

**3. The File Design Environment    22**

File Design    22
Adding New Application Programs to an Existing
    Application Area    26
Adding a New Application Area to an Existing System    37
Inherent Problems in File Processing    40
Today's Data Management Problems    42

**4. Data Base Design Environment    45**

Storage Reduction    46
File Consolidation    48

Data Independence   58

Data Base Security   64

Evolutionary Growth   69

Data Recovery   75

Programmer Productivity   79

## 5. Highlights of the Data Base Era   89

Types of Data Processing Systems   89

Data Base Administration   92

Educational Criteria in Areas of Specialization   95

The Functional Flow of Information   101

A Point of Clarification   105

## Index   107

# Preface

In today's computer world, we are witnessing a revolutionary trend in data processing strategy emerging (1) from single file access to "shared" data base design, (2) from report generation to "on-line" retrieval, and (3) from implementing a single application program to the planning of interrelated application areas. In essence, we've moved into a new era of optimized resources and integrated systems, requiring long-range analysis and commitments on the corporate level.

This "new era" has placed us in a highly complex environment, requiring detail evaluation in many areas. Some of these areas include (1) analyzing "total" data processing requirements, (2) evaluating software products, and (3) planning integrated systems. While each area has its complications, software evaluation deserves special attention. This phase alone may range from six months to three years, requiring travel, seminars, course attendance, and a host of in-house discussions.

Why are these complications present in our new data processing era? While novelties do present challenges, other contributing factors include:

The lack of introductory material on data base/data communication systems.

The lack of introductory material for each program product (e.g., indicating features and their intended usage).

The lack of documented guidelines for evaluating integrated data processing requirements (e.g., matching those requirements with program product features).

Because these factors were present in the late 1960s, some installations are now committed to systems they do not like, while others are faced with delayed target dates, doubled manpower estimates, and various forms of implementation bottlenecks. "Being pulled up by the boot straps" can best summarize many war stories told in data processing circles.

Because of these war stories, corporate executives have requested visits to installations where the proposed system has been installed. While their strategy is plausible, it often leads to a dead end. Most users cannot afford the time required for frequent one-day seminars. And so, software evaluation doesn't get any easier, newly committed installations usually reinvent the wheel, and the process usually costs more than anticipated.

Having worked with DB/DC (Data Base/Data Communication) systems since the late 1960s, I have seen repeated errors in our analysis of implementation bottlenecks. Some think that bottlenecks stem from oversimplifying the mission (shortcomings in executive plans or the lack of a plan). Others say that problems stem from the lack of previous experience (to be expected in a new era). Through consulting experience, I found that most problems stemmed from "assuming" features that were not there. Without knowing the total system, we cannot see the forest for the trees.

In many instances, we try to address these problems through classroom attendance. In industry, however, tuition fees usually average $300 in addition to standard travel allowances. While only a few students can attend, some find that courses tend to emphasize "how little you know" as opposed to enlightening each student. Are we really that unprepared or is "genius" required to understand these new systems?

As an educator, I find the answer to be no to both answers. Classes are often conducted without a conceptual (introductory) base for material. This is equivalent to placing a fifth-grade student in a senior class. And, let's face it, the student (be he programmer, manager, or analyst) does not have the right perspective to understand the course or apply these skills immediately.

To highlight this point, assume that introductory material on today's DB/DC systems would begin as follows:

A software product is a program that automates some in-house code that is "common" among your application programs. It therefore saves you coding and debugging time. Let's look at these time-saving features. . . .

In most instances, the teaching approach to this kind of information would begin at a much higher level of technical jargon. Oftentimes, acronyms and other program product terms are not properly introduced. These situations, coupled with a void in good introductory material, has created a "fog" index in systems. And frequently we find ourselves knowing implementation techniques without understanding the many ways in which we employ features.

When I first encountered this, I was exposed to approximately 100 acronyms during a one-week course. Moreover, the course convinced me that I didn't know anything. So I read every available book and scheduled time for computer exercises. Within one year I found myself being consulted by managers, programmers, and planners. One day, however, I was politely insulted. After a one-hour session in which I had displayed many illustrations, a manager asked, "Yes, but what does the system do for me in general terms?" From that day forward I realized an important factor. A basic understanding of total system characteristics had to be derived, and we could only derive this information by using system features in systems design, application programming, and systems programming—unless, of course, introductory material on the subject was available. With this in mind, I was prompted to write a *primer* on data base systems.

Now, a primer is defined in Webster's as a small introductory book. And this definition is important because it sets the stage for the objective of this publication. This publication introduces data base features and their intended usage in an effort to answer this question: "What is it and what does it do for me?"

The answers are not references to data base systems because I feel you can call your local salesman and obtain up-to-date descriptions on any program product. There is no effort to sell data base. There is only an effort to define data base features common among data base systems like TOTAL, System 2000, IDMS, IMS, and a host of other products.

Now you may ask if the features are not related to data base products, "How does this publication help me?"

First of all, there are many data base systems being marketed today. And most of these systems use common terminology, like data independence and data security. Yet, the extent of data independence may differ from one product to another. By reading about data independence in this publication, you will know the extent of independence—and its enhancements to your installation. I believe this approach to data base features is far more beneficial to you. If you are in the process of selecting a data base system, for example, you will want the comfort of knowing

*You made the right decision!*

because this publication will have equipped you with the necessary information to evaluate data base systems. I believe that this alone is a priceless asset when we think of the dollars and manpower requirements.

Secondly, the techniques used in most data base systems are rather intricate, and a good overview will expedite the learning process. Stated differently, if I know the general characteristics of one car, I know the general characteristics of all cars—regardless of their manufacturers. And knowing the general characteristics of data base systems makes it easier to understand the details at the mechanical level.

Thirdly, the data base era represents a new concept in data management. As opposed to one file being dedicated to one application, we can merge files into a "common" structure. When we start sharing data processing resources at this level, we should define each functional area of responsibility and the relationship between each function. Considerable text material has been provided along this line of thought for two reasons: You will have fewer implementation problems with data base systems, and you could improve your productivity in a file design environment.

# 1 The Data Base Era

Suddenly we are off and running into a whole new ball game in the data processing industry. And this time, we call it the *data base era*. Fortunately, the data base era represents a new approach to storing data. That is, files can be consolidated, consolidated files can be shared, and shared files (or data bases) can result in an astronomical cost savings. Unfortunately, we have been baffled because the cost savings areas haven't been identified and fringe benefits haven't been stated. So let's put the horse back in front of the cart and start from the beginning.

There are many questions that we could ask about the data base era. While some could range from simple to complex, *our first* approach to examining this era should be sheer practicality: We should want to know the basic features of data base systems as they relate to our data processing environments. Now, this excludes technical jargon and voluminous manuals that give microscopic details. This excludes seminars and classroom presentations on coding techniques and performance considerations. After all, these things will come in the proper sequence of events. What we want is concise (and down to earth) answers on the following questions:

What are the basic features of a system?

How do these features improve our operating environment?

What are some of the cost-savings areas?

What are the education guidelines?

Unfortunately, these questions have been suppressed through sophisticated hedging techniques, called "new terminology." To go around this problem, we've turned to users who have installed data base systems. This leads into a blind alley because few installations have time for frequent executive seminars. Others discuss data base applications and implementation bottlenecks. And even the implementation bottlenecks do not help us when stated microscopically:

> We lost two months when our PSBs and DBDs were inconsistent—and another six months when our data base was destroyed without a log tape backup.

And the brave souls who would ask "What's a PSB?" would probably discover that a PSB is composed of one or more PCBs, each of which references a given DBD that authorizes the application program to access segment occurrences. If the PSB and DBD do not name identical members, than the application program terminates with a "bad" status code return from DL/I.

As you can see, we know even less about the two-month delay. Having lost the battle for practical answers and being wounded by microscopic details in installation seminars, we turn to isolated applications. That is, we try to locate an installation that has installed a specific application (such as General Ledgers). Thus, if the Ford Motor Company has installed Data Base X, then other car manufacturers can install the same system. If United Airlines has installed Data Base System XL, then perhaps other airlines can install the same system. And the list goes on and on.

If we approach the data base era from this angle, we are doomed from the start because the problems in Company X may be different from the problems in Company B, since implementation procedures may vary with each factor. Then, again, we would seek another measurement. So, let's erase any knowledge we have acquired on the data base era. Let's start off fresh in mind and spirit. We will take one step at a time using everyday English to cover the data base era.

What is the data base era? The data base era introduces a new way of storing (and accessing) processed data. That is, installations accumulate data on files and these files are processed by application programs. Over a period of time, installations design more and more files as they implement new applications. The data base era says:

> Let's examine your collection of files and determine better ways of storing data. Since you have duplicated items (e.g., part numbers) in different files, let's devise a technique that eliminates many of these duplicated items.

In other words, *the data base era represents the consolidation of files*. Once consolidated, you can reduce input/output (I/O) devices, update processing, and file designs. Once consolidated, you can eliminate backup copies. And once consolidated, you have a cleaner operating environment.

Most vendors of data base systems have designed *general-purpose systems*. These systems were designed to handle any kind of data, be it the part number, manufacturing process(es), inventory status, or personnel records. In many ways, these general-purpose data base systems can be viewed as extensions to an operating system. First, however, let's review the major differences between second-generation and third-generation computers. If you are already familiar with these differences, please skip to the next section (Operating System Extensions).

Initially, computers were installed with minimum software support. That is, we received little (if any) preprogrammed services that were distributed with the computer. In some cases, our software support consisted of compilers * that were distributed in card form. As I recall those days, we'd keep rows and rows of card files containing several versions of each application program because the card reader (our only source of input) sometimes mutilated (digested) cards at the most inopportune time. If this occurred, we'd have to read in large compiler decks and wait patiently for the card read/punch unit to finally punch the executable deck. Using the punched program, we would then read the application program and all its input data in card format. Imagine the laborious task of stacking 5,000 cards into the card hopper. These operations are diagrammed in Figs. 1.1 and 1.2.

As computer manufacturers improved their software and hardware, many of the operator responsibilities were automated. Application programs and files could be accessed from disk or tape simply by reading a few control cards.

In addition to automating these services, these computing systems were equipped with input/output (I/O) channels that could process their own I/O programs. That is, the operating system could issue an I/O command to the channel, and while the channel was reading (or writing) a record, the operating system could start another operation. This enhancement allowed the operating system to schedule multiple application programs (see Fig. 1.3). When Program A issued

---

* Compilers are programs that convert application program source code (e.g., COBOL; FORTRAN, etc.) into executable machine language.

**Figure 1.1.** Earlier efforts in data processing environment consisted of laborious operator tasks and voluminous card files

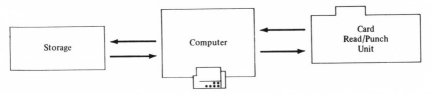

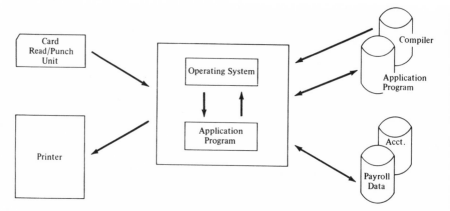

**Figure 1.2.** Using Operating Systems to perform services that were completed manually

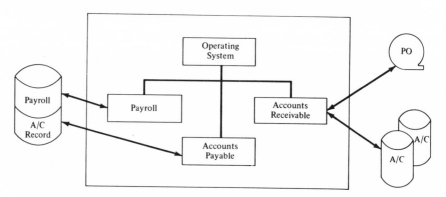

**Figure 1.3.** Using an Operating System to share hardware resources among application programs

an input/output request, the operating system issued a channel command and transferred control to Program B. The channel performed the input/output operation while Program B executed application code. Thus, by automating operating systems, we were able to share computer and file resources with application programs that were executing concurrently.

## Operating System Extensions

With hardware/software improvements came new applications. Instead of implementing one clerical step (such as student registration or payroll), we could implement interrelated clerical procedures within an application—for example,

**Figure 1.4.**

Student Registration, Student Enrollment, and Geographical Distributions (see Fig. 1.4). In doing so, we found many interwoven complexities that could only be handled by a larger data processing staff. Our staff grew in size, but we still had not solved the problems: Each employee assumed the role of application analysis, data gathering, data analysis, program design, and program implementation, which seemed impractical.

To expedite implementation, we divided this process into functional areas of specialization (Fig. 1.5). Like car manufacturers, each employee performed a specific function that related to the completion of a finished product. The *systems designer* analyzed total data processing requirements (for a given application) and divided them into subsets. The *application analyst* analyzed his subset and divided it into application program requirements. The application analyst gave the application program requirements (specification) to *application programmers* who were responsible for writing and testing the code.

One specific task (denoted by B in Fig. 1.5) might encompass a host of interrelated activities. In registration, for example, we have to consult admissions

**Figure 1.5.** Due to complex (and interwoven) clerical chores that were too voluminous to be handled by one employee, the implementation process was divided into functional areas of specialization.

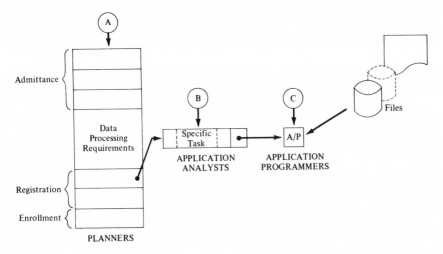

records to be sure a student has been authorized to attend the university in order to let him register. Since registration includes course selections, we have to retain information on the status of each course enrollment. This complex procedure can be summarized as follows:

*Registration Procedure*
Verify student entry.

Check tuition payment records.

Validate student classification.

Accept or reject course request based on student classification and course availability.

*Registration Maintenance*
Update course enrollment information and remove course from list when full.

Print message if removed course is required (e.g., English 101 for Freshmen).

*Registration Reports*
List all students and their courses alphabetically.

List all courses and enrolled students alphabetically by course.

Generate the same reports above, categorizing by student majors (e.g., Physics; Engineering, etc.).

In each of the above requirements, the application analyst examines detailed information on each step and documents program specifications (Fig. 1.6). Each program specification is given to an application programmer. Since application

**Figure 1.6.** To expedite coding, the application programmer is given program specifications which include processing requirements, report formats (results of code) and file formats (input data used to calculate or print report).

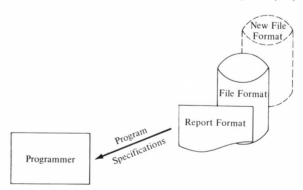

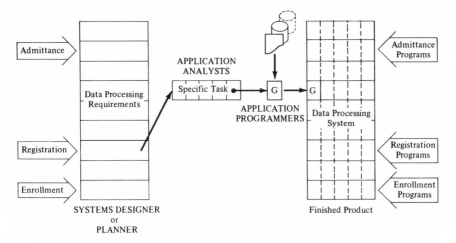

**Figure 1.7.** The Registration System is a composite of application programs that went through the cycle of system analysis (planners), detail analysis (application analysts), and coding (application programmers).

programming had its own complexities, the application analyst removes external (environmental) complexities in order for the coding process to be expedited.

When each application program has been written and tested, the application analyst makes sure the series of application programs will complete the clerical steps he has been given. By combining all the application programs assigned by different application analysts, we have a registration system (Fig. 1.7) that replaces clerical steps. In other words, the finished product matches the design specifications of the planners.

As you might imagine, the details of an application (such as registration, accounts payable, purchasing, etc.) can become so complex that we find ourselves needing two levels of expertise for our data processing staff. Purchasing, for example, can be implemented. To do this, however, our data processing staff needs the same in-depth knowledge of purchasing procedures as the employees in the Purchasing Department. For this reason, installations have defined several data processing departments, each being assigned a chartered responsibility for a given application. Mr. Brown, for example, is a data processing manager of Personnel Systems. He has a staff of planners, application analysts, and application programmers, who are responsible for designing, implementing, and maintaining the programs that service employees in the Personnel Department. Mr. Williams (manager of Inventory Control) has an equivalent data processing staff that maintains programs to service employees in the Production Control Department. By assigning permanent applications to each department, we developed a functional data processing organization.

As time progressed, we had implemented a number of systems. Unfortunately, we often treated each application as if it were an independent unit of the corporation. Our purchasing system (managed by Mr. Jones) handled purchase orders (as it should have), while our inventory system (managed by Mr. Williams) handled the inventory status of parts (as it should have). But if we were to perform corporate analysis on the contents of files (and the functions of application programs), we would probably find the following results:

### Corporate Analysis of Purchasing
### and Inventory Control Systems

*File Contents*
85% duplicate storage of parts information among the two systems.

*Back-up Files*
50% backup of equivalent information.

*Application Programs*
85% excessive update processing for equivalent information among systems.

30% excessive retrievals (reports) for equivalent information.

Now, let's take a closer look at the amount of duplicate data among data processing systems (Fig. 1.8). We know that the purchasing system records the parts ordered on each PO (purchase order). The inventory control system records both the parts ordered and parts on hand. In both systems, we have the part number, part description, unit of measure, quantity ordered, and scheduled delivery date. These items are repeated several times in many different files. When parts are delivered at the receiving dock, both systems have to be updated to reflect the "new" quantity on hand (inventory control) and pending shipments (purchasing system).

We see that we now have two different update programs (one per system) that update the same information in different files. And we have two backup files for the same information in two different systems. In other words, the data processing systems that process the same type of data (e.g., parts) also store the same type of data in their files. Only the usage changes.

On close examination, we may find ourselves paying an excessive overhead in data processing facilities to process the same information in different ways for different application areas. Unfortunately, this overhead isn't always apparent. Since our data processing systems satisfy requirements, we have found little (if any) reason to examine the relationship of data within the corporation. To detect

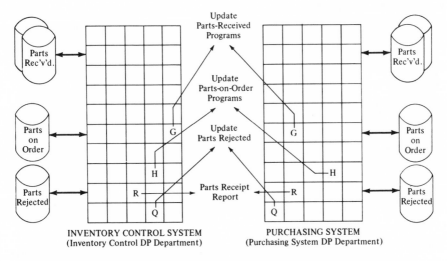

**Figure 1.8.** When examining application areas that store the same type of data, duplicate information among files, duplicate update programs and duplicate back-up files for the same information are found.

this overhead, we would have to analyze the files (and application programs) among interrelated application areas. That is, we would have to choose two systems that processed the same type of information. After a careful evaluation of these systems, we would be able to identify (Fig. 1.8) the degree of duplicate files and application programs.

To highlight this point, let's examine a familiar environment—our local bank. Most commercial banks, for example, handle checking accounts, savings accounts, personal loans, and mortgages. While each of these constitutes an application area, there are some banking customers who are associated with two or more of these areas. For example (Fig. 1.9), Mr. Smith has his savings and checking accounts at the First National Bank of Highland. When he purchased his car, he acquired a car loan from the same bank. Now Mr. Smith's name and other personal data appear in files belonging to savings accounts, checking accounts, and personal loans.

**Figure 1.9.** Multiple copies of customer data among application areas

If Mr. Smith made several deposits into his checking account last month, chances are that his name appears several times (once per deposit). This creates multiple Smith entries within the checking account files as well.

While operating systems have automated manual operator functions, data base (DB) systems have a similar objective; to consolidate data entries among files. That is, data base systems are designed to manage shared files (Fig. 1.10) if you convert (reformat) them according to the guidelines software companies specify.

In other words, a single copy of Smith's personal data (name, address, marital status, etc.) can be "shared" among the Savings Accounts, Checking Accounts and Personal Loan areas.

*A data base environment represents a consolidation of information that is usually processed by two or more applications.* In this environment, we may continue to implement new applications, and even call them "systems." Instead of designing independent files for each new application, we need only design the application programs (Fig. 1.11). These programs can access information stored in our "shared" data base.

By examining Fig. 1.12, you will find that we have duplicate resources in both files and application programs. Since programs G, H, R, and Q perform the same function on the same type of data in both systems, we can consolidate both the files and application programs (as shown in Fig. 1.13). By the same token, there may be clerical steps required to prepare update transaction cards in two different application areas. We could consolidate the update activities of Program G in both systems, replacing it with $G_1$ (Fig. 1.13), and reduce our clerical steps. The Purchasing Department, for example, could prepare all the update transaction on parts received: Program $G_1$ would be executed and the Parts Receipt File would be updated. Now, the "most recent" information on parts

**Figure 1.10.** Sharing a single copy of Smith's personal data among application areas

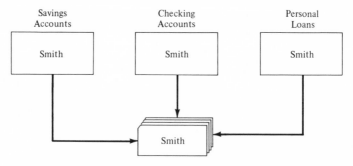

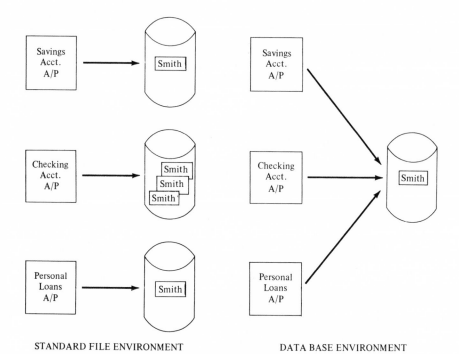

STANDARD FILE ENVIRONMENT          DATA BASE ENVIRONMENT

**Figure 1.11.** A comparison of file resources used in two different environments: standard file design versus data base design

**Figure 1.12.** Examining the resources within two data processing systems to determine the ones that can be consolidated without losing data processing services

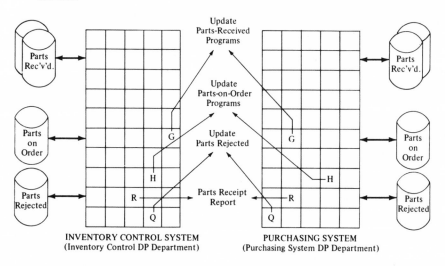

11

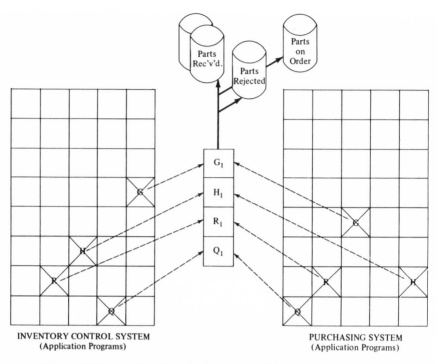

**Figure 1.13.** Using a Data Base System to consolidate data processing resources common to both systems. In this case, we eliminate four files and application programs.

received would become available to both the inventory control and purchasing systems at the same time. Thus, we reduce storage (by consolidating common files), reduce application programs (by eliminating duplicate update programs), and reduce clerical steps (by limiting transaction preparation to one application area) and improve data reliability (by sharing the most recent information with both application areas). All these advantages become possible when we consolidate resources that can be shared among application areas.

In a data base environment, a data base system acts as a manager of its data bases. To perform its job, the data base system must be executed with the application program(s) that access the data bases it manages, as diagrammed in Fig. 1.14.

In a data base environment, your application programs would be submitted to DP operations for execution per usual. During execution, however, the operating system would load the data base system, and your application program. The application program can execute any instructions (per usual) until it wants data

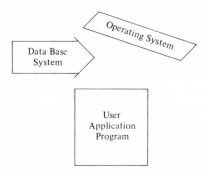

**Figure 1.14.** When using a data base, the Data Base System must reside in storage with the application program.

from the data base. At this point, the data base system gains control and handles the data base request. Afterward, data base information is passed to the application program and it regains control. This process is continued until the application program terminates. We thus have two new data processing resources:

*Data Base System:* A collection of application programs that are distributed in a software package. (Since the software is designed by a vendor, we call them "systems programs.") These systems programs are designed to handle data stored in a data base. That is, they update and/or retrieve information stored in the data base when requests are issued.

*Data Base:* A collection of files that have been consolidated and reformatted.

In summary, a data base system contains all the necessary systems programs required to service input/output requests against the data bases they manage. By doing so, they act like an extension to the operating system—interfacing between the application programs (that request data base information) and the data bases they manage (Fig. 1.15). This does not impair the services performed by the operating system, nor does it restrict code in the application program. You may execute programs using standard files concurrently with programs using a mixture of files and data bases. So, let's add the data base system to your processing environment.In essence, *general purpose data base (DB) systems are service programs designed to coordinate and consolidate files.* And, like operating systems, data base systems can be used by any installation desirous of file consolidation. The type of installation (Fig. 1.16) is secondary to DB systems, just as the type of application program is secondary to an operating system. It simply schedules resources.

At this point in our discussion, we know very little about a data base system

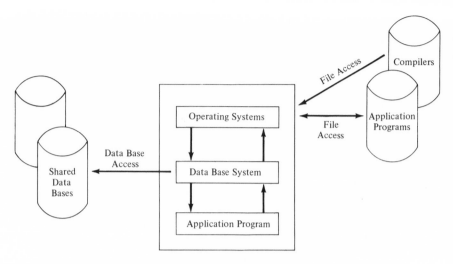

**Figure 1.15.** Using Operating Systems for hardware management and Data Base Systems for "shared" file (data base) management

or the features contained therein. But let's review what we do know. We know that the data base era has brought about a new concept in file design that can best be summarized as *file consolidation*. We know that a data base system contains a series of systems programs that manage their data bases by interfacing between the application programs that access them. We know that most data base systems do not replace application programming, nor do they restrict application code. We also know that we need not restructure our data processing organization to implement new systems, since we are simply sharing data bases among application areas.

Knowing this, let's review the remainder of the text. First we will review "assumed" terms, that is, terms used frequently but rarely defined. (If you are familiar with these terms, please bypass this section.) Then, we will use the next three sections to compare current file design techniques with data base design techniques. These sections are interrelated as follows: We developed an assembly-line approach to implementation when we discovered the interwoven complexities within applications. By assigning a specific application to each data processing department, we expedited implementation for many applications, and over time we accumulated many systems and their files. By examining our collection of files and systems, we would find duplicate resources.

While this explanation of "duplicate resources" allows us to see the need for consolidation, we have vastly underestimated the number of duplicate resources. With implementation came implementation bottlenecks, and with im-

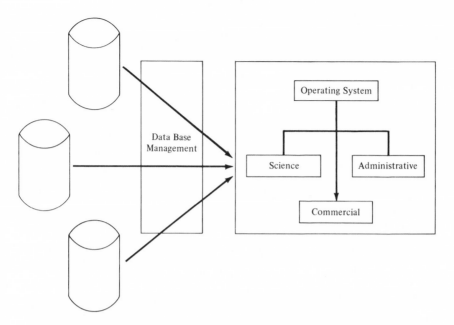

**Figure 1.16.** A general-purpose data base system handles data from application areas, just like an Operating System schedules diversified application programs.

plementation bottlenecks came excessive resources within one application area. The third chapter describes the origin of today's bottlenecks and illustrates the degree of excessive resources within one system.

In "Inherent Problems in File Processing," we will extend this discussion by examining the accumulation of systems and files. After unveiling the hidden problems, we will resolve them by employing the features of a good data base system. In the final section you will find a specific feature and its benefits. And where appropriate, you will find a list of cost-savings areas for each feature.

Since no data base system is an end-all-ills-unto-itself, we will discuss the shortcomings of some features. Using customer contacts over the years, I have included customer recommendations which I feel should be weighed: If data base systems did everything one could imagine, we would probably allocate the entire computer to the system, leaving little room for our applications. We really need to know our data processing requirements (of the data base system) and implement accordingly.

In *The Data Base Design Environment* you will find the *cause and effect* of today's shortcomings in the file environment and potential shortcomings in the data base environment. Instead of recommending more data base features, I've pinpointed the source of our problems and recommended some software tools that help us identify data base requirements and manage data processing resources. In the last section you will find recommended education guidelines for the data base environment.

And finally, in the last chapter I have included implementation guidelines with some skepticism. Most people think of implementation guidelines as a step-by-step procedure for data base implementation. On the contrary, we simply cannot implement a good data base without first analyzing the data processing resources. That is, we need to analyze all the files and application programs *today* before designing a replacement for the files *tomorrow*. Even if you implement a subset of your total resources (such as purchasing and inventory control), the subset must be carefully studied prior to implementation.

Having read these chapters you will have a better understanding of the data base era and the subtle (and often hidden) problems in the assembly line of implementation. From this, you should be able to avoid many of the implementation bottlenecks in a file environment, and improve your data processing resources in a data base environment. In either case, you will be more prepared for the data network systems that await us farther down the "road of future systems."

# 2 Definition of Terms

In today's data processing world, we find ourselves surrounded with terms that each of us assumes the other person knows. As opposed to making this assumption in the very beginning, let's take a few moments to define a few terms and acronyms. As opposed to placing these terms in alphabetical order, let's review them as they were introduced into the data processing world. If you are familiar with them, please bypass this section.

## EAM Equipment

Our first attempt to automate the manual processing of data dates back to the 1940s when Hollerith introduced an automatic technique to analyze data collected by the Bureau of the Census. EAM (Electronic Accounting Machines) consisted of a family of units that were manually wired to perform a function. Familiar units (Fig. 2.1) would include the "Interpreters" (to print the contents of punched cards in specific places on the card (e.g., telephone bill). "Sorters" placed a deck of cards in a given sequence. "Reproducers" reproduced card decks, and "Accounting Machines," such as the 407, could be wired to add, subtract, and format reports. To perform a given service, each unit had control panels, which were handwired by EAM personnel.

## File/Data Set

When we started with EAM equipment, we devised techniques to represent items of information on a punched card. We called each item by a field name and assigned each field name a specific location on the card (Fig. 2.2). Since each

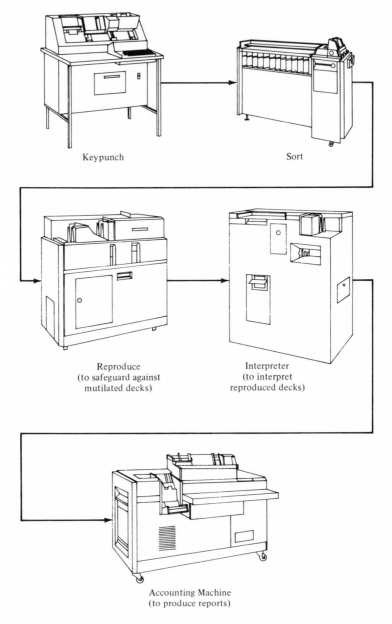

Keypunch                    Sort

Reproduce                   Interpreter
(to safeguard against       (to interpret
mutilated decks)            reproduced decks)

Accounting Machine
(to produce reports)

**Figure 2.1.** Hollerith's EAM system

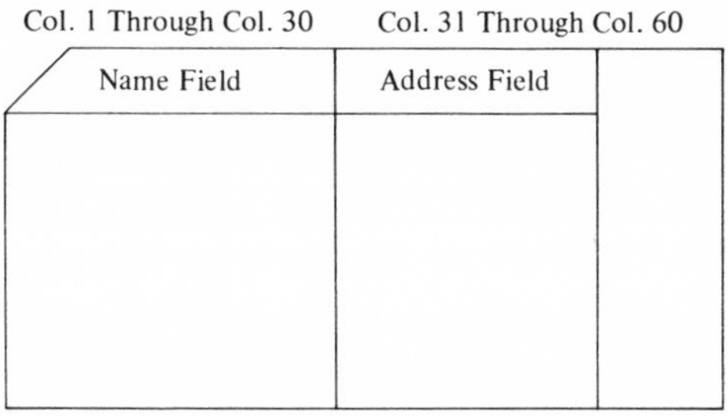

Col. 1 Through Col. 30      Col. 31 Through Col. 60

| Name Field | Address Field | |
|---|---|---|
| | | |

**Figure 2.2.** Punched card

entry of information had specific field locations, we used the word "format" to reference the layout of its card. Thus, the format told us what items were to be punched and where to punch them.

The terms used above are summarized as:

*Format:* The card layout, indicating the fields and their location.

*Field:* One or more columns reserved for a specific item on the card.

*Item:* The information being punched on the card (e.g., name, address, sex, etc.).

## Application Program (A/P)

With both second-generation and third-generation computers, we replaced EAM-type wired panels with precoded program logic called "application programming" (A/P). You will see later that A/P represents application program and/or application programmer.

When second-generation computers were introduced, we found ourselves using the terms "record" and "file." *A record is one complete entry of information.*

In EAM days, we used punched cards that were limited to 80 columns per card. With second- and third-generation computers, we received new input/output devices that allowed us to define the length of an entry. Payroll entries, for example, could have record entries 175 columns long, while a shipment record would contain only 75 columns. Thus, a record became one complete entry of information with a unique format (Fig. 2.3).

In Fig. 2.3 we have an employee master record, 159 columns long. Since this record is stored on tape or disk, we say it has 159 positions.

Records belonging to the same application with the same format can be stored on the same input/output device. The collection of records is called a *file:*

FORMAT

| | | |
|---|---|---|
| EMPLOYEE NO. | 6 | 1–6 |
| EMPLOYEE NAME | 30 | 7–36 |
| DEPARTMENT | 2 | 37–38 |
| DATE HIRED | 6 | 39–44 |
| LINE 1 | 25 | 45–69 |
| LINE 2 | 25 | 70–94 |
| LINE 3 | 25 | 95–119 |
| LINE 4 | 25 | 120–144 |
| GROSS SALARY | 6 | 145–150 |
| SALARY CLASS | 3 | 151–153 |
| AUTH DATE | 6 | 154–159 |

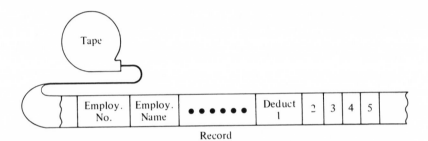

Record

**Figure 2.3.**

**Figure 2.4.**

| Era | Item | Space for Item | Collection of Items | Collection of Records |
|---|---|---|---|---|
| Punched Card | Item | Columns and fields | Unit Record | Card deck |
| Second Generation | Item | Columns (card) Positions (I/O device) Fields | Record Block | Card deck Files |
| Third Generation | Data elements | Columns (card) Positions (I/O device) | Record Block volume | Data sets Files |

*Record:* A collection of fields that have specific locations assigned to them.

*File:* A collection of records with the same format (e.g., an employee master file would contain one record per employee).

As we progress toward third-generation computers, we find that their operating systems have records stored on systems files. Instead of differentiating between systems files and customer files, we introduce two new terms: data elements and data sets. A *data element* is an item stored in a record, be it system or customer resource. A *data set* is a collection of records with the same format, be it system or customer resource.

While many customers use third-generation computers, the terms *files* and *fields* are used frequently. Therefore, this publication uses the mixture of terms shown in Fig. 2.4.

# 3 The File Design Environment

In this chapter we spend some time looking at file design as it relates to data base design. This does not include the intricate details of file design relative to file access and access frequency. Instead, we focus on the general characteristics of file design as it relates to (1) adding new application programs to an existing application area, (2) adding new application areas to an existing system, and (3) data processing overhead that may result from treating application areas as separate entities. From these we can understand the data processing enhancements that can be derived from a *good data base system*.

## File Design

Traditionally, we have used three types of file design (formats) to process data in a data processing environment. They include (1) the fixed-length record, (2) the variable-length record, and (3) the undefined record. The *fixed-length record format* is a file composed of record entries that adhere to a fixed length. In other words, a file composed of 1,000 records has each record formatted the same way, as in Fig. 3.1.

**Figure 3.1.** Vendor's name and address file composed of 150 column record entries for each vendor

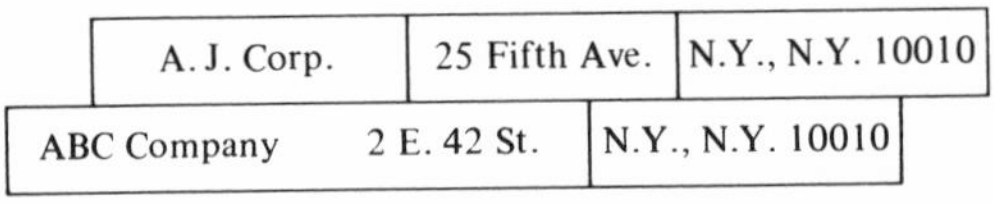

| A. J. Corp. | 25 Fifth Ave. | N.Y., N.Y. 10010 |
|-------------|---------------|------------------|
| ABC Company | 2 E. 42 St. | N.Y., N.Y. 10010 |

In Fig. 3.1, the vendor file has been designed for a fixed-length record format (150 positions long) with field assignments for the vendor name (positions 1–50); street (positions 51–100), and City/State (positions 101–150). Each vendor entry is entered in the same format within the fixed-length record design.

The *variable-length record format* is a file composed of records that can vary in length. That is, each record within this file can be entered in a different (unique) length. Before illustrating a file containing variable-length records, let's describe an application that could use a variable-length format. Suppose, for example, the Purchasing Department had a need to track the dollars spent with each vendor by PO (purchase order number). By storing the vendor's name and address, the PO number, and the dollars committed or paid, a monthly report can be generated.

The variable-length format design is appropriate for this application because of the variation in purchase order placement. Snow Removal Service, Inc., for example, may be contracted annually at a fixed amount for removing snow, and would therefore receive only one purchase order from the Purchasing Department. Cafeteria Orders Company, however, has a one-year contract to supply food, using a monthly purchase order. Suppliers of manufacturing parts, however, may receive as many as 2,000 purchase orders per year. Since the number of purchase orders placed with a given vendor can vary, the use of variable-length records is practical.

With the variable-length record, we can define a format for each type (segment) of data. For the Purchasing Department's requirement, we can define a format for the vendor's name and address information, and a second format for PO information (Fig. 3.2). To do this, let's retain the 150-position format for vendor information and define a 16-position format for PO information. Now the vendor information can be entered, and each new PO entry can be appended to the end of the vendor information (Fig. 3.3).

The variable-length record is not limited to two formats as previously described. We can add as many formats as required for the application. If we realize the need for adding new formats to an existing file, however, we should plan ahead. To do this, we should design for application program independence by placing a code in each type of format. The vendor address file, for example, con-

**Figure 3.2.** Defining a unique format for PO Number and Dollars Committed/Paid information, which will be labeled PO dollars

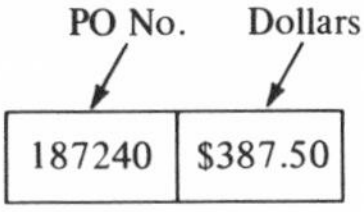

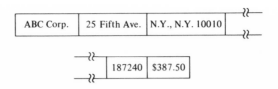

**Figure 3.3.** Adding new PO Dollars to the end of its vendor entry each time a new PO is placed

tains two types of formats: address data and dollars data. We can design for data independence by placing a code in each format. By using identification codes (Fig. 3.4), we can add another format to the record without revising application programs that do not need to access the new information. To highlight this point, suppose the Accounting Department requested a monthly report, called ''Vendor Payments,'' that reflected the invoice number and the dollars paid to each vendor. Since this data processing requirement can be satisfied, in part, with the above information, we need only add the invoice number and dollars paid.

To add the information required by the Accounting Department, we can design another format. The format would include the invoice number (six positions) and dollars paid (ten positions). This 16-position format is the same length as PO dollars. This, however, will not create problems within other application programs if we have used codes to distinguish one format type from another format type, as in Fig. 3.5.

Using a variable-length record like Fig. 3.5, we can process multiple application programs that use a single (common) file. As illustrated in Fig. 3.6, the vendor address program, for example, can generate a vendor directory by processing format Type A. By doing so, a directory of each vendor and his address can be made available to the buyers within the Purchasing Department. The buyers could also obtain a monthly report of dollars paid or committed by executing the PO dollars program. This program would process format types A and B, generating a report containing the vendor's name, address, PO numbers and dollars (committed/paid). And, the Accounting Department could obtain its

**Figure 3.4.** Adding an identification code to each format type within a variable-length record

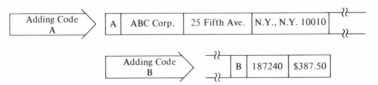

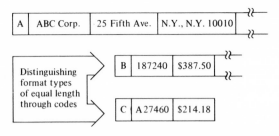

**Figure 3.5.** Using format-type codes to distinguish one data format from another with the same length of information

report by executing the PO payments program. This program would process formats types A and C, generating a report of dollars paid and invoice numbers for each vendor.

In summary, we often use the variable-length record to process entries that can vary in length. We can extend its usage by adding other types of data. By adding different types of data, we can share a file among application areas. Since each application program will process its types of data formats, we often use codes to distinguish one format type from another. In this way we can add new format types without revising the existing application programs. The existing application programs would change only (1) if they needed to process the new format types, or (2) if they were designed to process a maximum format size, but the new format types exceeded the "maximum" size. And since we code the maximum size within each application program, we often increase the maximum size in order to allow for future growth.

The undefined record format is a format in which the application program assumes full responsibility for processing. That is, the undefined record is

**Figure 3.6.** Using a variable-length format to share data among applications, such as Accounting and Purchasing application areas

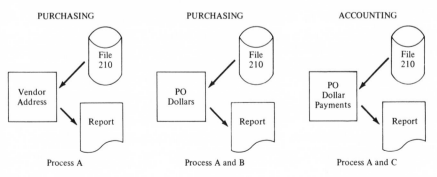

typically variable-length in design and employed wherever we would use a variable length record. The difference, however, resides in how the record is passed between the application program and the operating system. If the application program asked to READ a variable-length record, each READ would result in passing one format type to the application program (called "deblocking"). If an application program asked to READ an undefined record, each READ would result in passing all format types on the record to the application program. It then becomes the responsibility of the application programs to identify each type of data format within the record. And since this requires more application programming and debugging efforts, the undefined record is usually not employed in file design. For this reason, the undefined record will not be discussed in subsequent topics.

## Adding New Application Programs to an Existing Application Area

If we have already installed parts of an application area, we may find ourselves adding new application programs to that application area (Fig. 3.7). When this occurs, we may find ourselves needing to access data in existing files. To de-

**Figure 3.7.** Purchasing system. When adding a new application program to an existing application area, its data requirements may already exist on files.

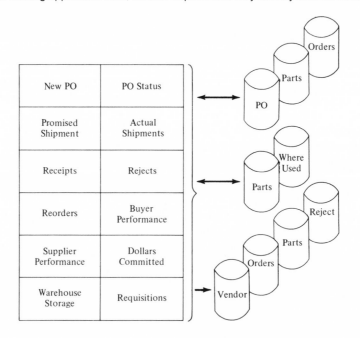

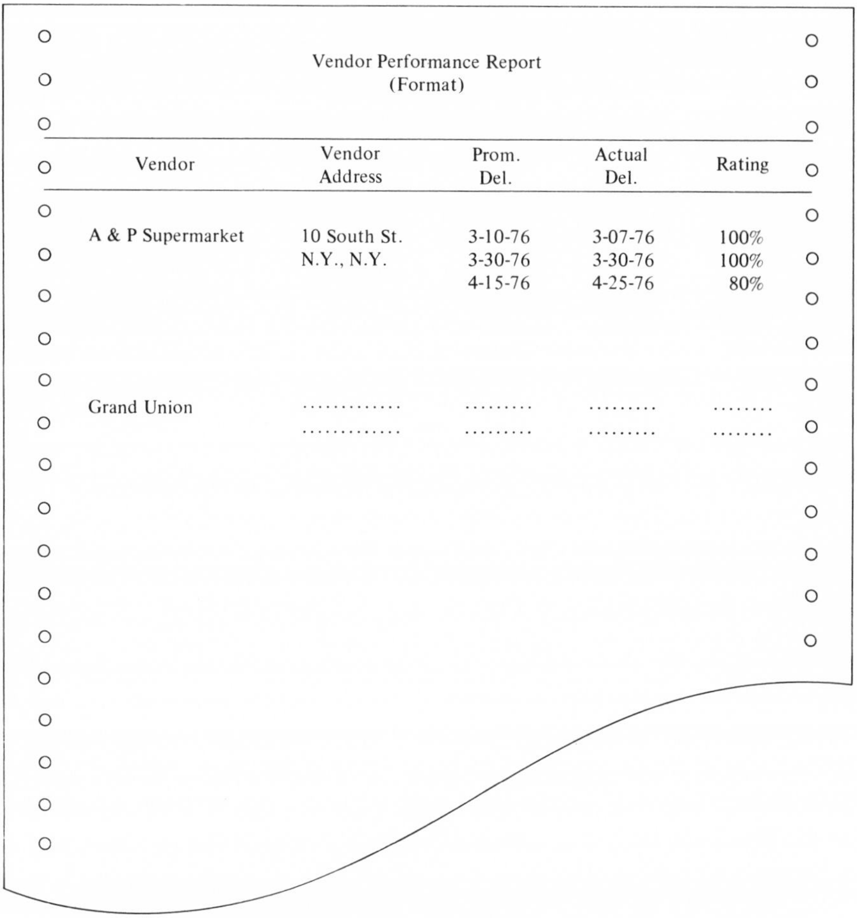

| Vendor | Vendor Address | Prom. Del. | Actual Del. | Rating |
|--------|---------------|-----------|-------------|--------|
| A & P Supermarket | 10 South St. N.Y., N.Y. | 3-10-76 3-30-76 4-15-76 | 3-07-76 3-30-76 4-25-76 | 100% 100% 80% |
| Grand Union | ............. ............. | ......... ......... | ......... ......... | ........ ........ |

*Vendor Performance Report (Format)*

**Figure 3.8.** Determining data element requirements by examining the information to be reported on the Vendor Performance Report

termine whether or not all the data exist on files, we need to examine the data element requirements for the new application program, as illustrated by Fig. 3.8.

Having obtained the data element requirements, we now have to identify the source (file or sources) where they can be found (see Fig. 3.9).

We may find that the data elements required for the new application program exist in three files. And the application program need only read the files, extract the information, and calculate the performance rating. After calculating the rating, it generates a report, as shown in Fig. 3.10.

After calculating the performance rating, the application program should

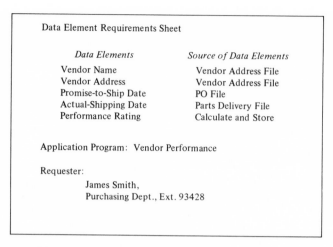

Data Element Requirements Sheet

| *Data Elements* | *Source of Data Elements* |
|---|---|
| Vendor Name | Vendor Address File |
| Vendor Address | Vendor Address File |
| Promise-to-Ship Date | PO File |
| Actual-Shipping Date | Parts Delivery File |
| Performance Rating | Calculate and Store |

Application Program:  Vendor Performance

Requester:

      James Smith,
      Purchasing Dept., Ext. 93428

**Figure 3.9.** When adding a new application program, we have to define its data element requirements and their source of input.

store the rating on a file for subsequent reports. And since the rating is related to each vendor, we will store the performance rating; promise-to-ship, and actual shipment with the vendor address file. Thus the storage of these data elements brings about the need to revise the design of the vendor address file.

The feasibility of file design revisions is contingent upon file design. That is, the complexity of revising a file design is based upon whether we designed a fixed-length or variable-length record. With a variable-length record design, we

**Figure 3.10.** The data element requirements for new application programs often exist on files.

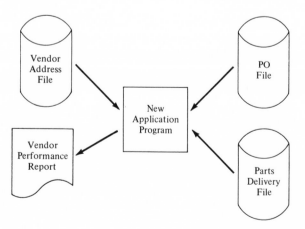

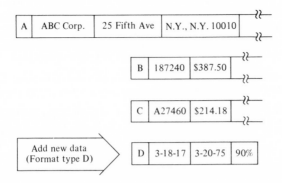

**Figure 3.11.** If a new application program requires data elements that do not exist, we can design a new format type within a variable-length record.

can add new data by designing a new format type (Fig. 3.11). In other words, we can add promise-to-deliver, actual delivery, and performance rating to the vendor address file as a new format type. Subsequent reports can be generated by processing format types A and D (Fig. 3.11).

If we have used format-type codes, then we need not revise existing application programs, unless the length of the new format type exceeds the maximum length of an existing format type. In other words, if the maximum length of an existing format type is 150 positions, and the new format type is 200 positions, then the existing application programs have to be revised to reflect the maximum of 200 positions. This is demonstrated in Fig. 3.12. If the new format type does not exceed the size of the largest format type within an existing file, we need only write an application program to "load" the new format-type data to the existing file. After the new data has been added, we may resume writing, testing and debugging (correcting errors within) the application program that is being added to the application area.

If a file was designed for a variable-length records that do not contain format-type codes, then we may find ourselves revising all of the existing application programs, in addition to (1) loading the new format types and (2) writing the new application programs.

In summary, the feasibility of revising a file designed for variable-length records is based on the usage of format-type codes. If format-type codes were employed, and if the new format type does not exceed the maximum length, then we can focus on the efforts required to add the new application program. Existing application programs need not be revised unless their programming requirements have changed. If, on the other hand, format-type codes were not employed, we have to change the existing application programs in order to revise the file design they access.

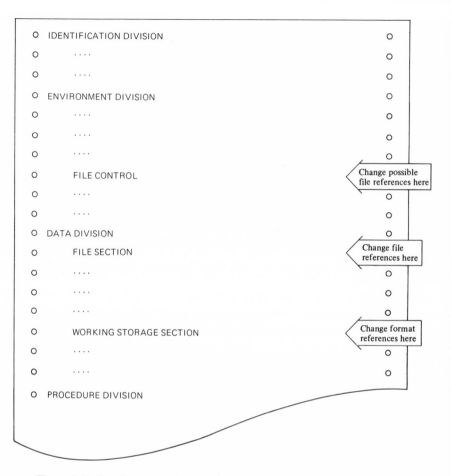

**Figure 3.12.** Denoting general areas of a COBOL application program must be revised when files are changed. Otherwise, the Operating System will cancel the program

If the file has been designed for fixed-length records, we would have to perform the following checklist of events:

Re-create the file by writing an application program to read each record; revise its format, and write each record on a new file.

Revise all the application programs that access the revised file.

Add the new data to the revised file format.

Proceed to add the new application program through coding, testing, and debugging.

The reason for re-creating the file is based on the way in which most operating systems store fixed-length records. Whether we increase the size of the records or decrease their size, the operating systems do not permit this type of revision on the input/output device. To change the format, then, we have to write an application program that reads the "old" version and revises it, and then write the "new" version on a new file.

All application programs that access the old version have file-dependent attributes coded within each application program. Again, we would have to revise each application program in corresponding areas as shown in Fig. 3.13.

Since the cost of these file design revisions could result in a six-month manpower effort for a given application program (with the exception of variable-length records with format-type codes), let's examine some alternatives to file design revisions. Keep in mind, again, that we are only examining cases where new application programs require data elements, some of which exist on files and others of which must be made available.

Since a six-month delay is somewhat impractical, let's examine alternatives to file design revisions. Before doing so, however, let's examine the file (Fig. 3.14) that contains parts of the data required by the new application program.

Let's assume that the file (Fig. 3.14) contains an entry for each vendor that the Purchasing Department does business with. It is used to generate the vendor directory. And, the Purchasing Department has requirements for a vendor performance report. This report will contain a list of vendors, and a percentage indicating the performance of each vendor.

To determine a vendor's performance, the application program must compare the promise-to-deliver date with the actual-delivery date and rate the vendor by subtracting ten points for each two-week delay in delivery. To process this requirement, then, the application program needs access to the vendor's name and address, promise-to-deliver date, and actual delivery date. It can obtain the vendor's name and address from the vendor address file, and the delivery dates from the PO file. However, the PO file contains a vendor number, and the vendor address file contains the vendor's name (Fig. 3.15). In order for the application program to associate the vendor number with its vendor name, we need to build a bridge between these files. We could place the vendor number in the vendor address file, but that would require file design revisions. And since we are examining alternatives to file design revisions, let's examine a typical approach to this problem. We will build a vendor table, which will have fixed-length records containing the vendor number and vendor name (Fig. 3.16) for each vendor in the vendor directory.

Using the vendor table, then, an application program would read the PO file and obtain the vendor number. Using the vendor number, it would then read the

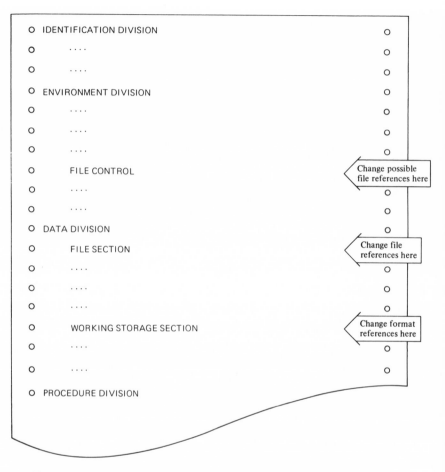

**Figure 3.13.** Denoting general areas of a COBOL application program must be revised when files are changed. Otherwise, the Operating System will cancel the program

vendor table and obtain the vendor name; using the vendor name, it would then obtain the vendor's name and address, as shown in Fig. 3.17.

The alternative to file design revisions, then, would require the design of new files (or tables), the usage of search fields, and a greater need to synchronize update activities. And the synchronization of updates says that each time a new

**Figure 3.14.**

| ABC Corp. | 15 Fifth Ave. | N.Y., N.Y. 10010 |

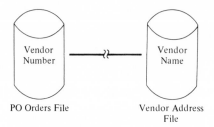

**Figure 3.15.**

**Figure 3.16.**

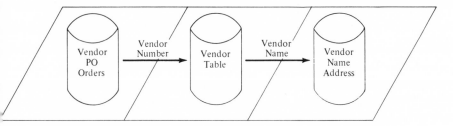

**Figure 3.17.** Using the new file to locate and obtain the vendor's name and address

vendor is added to the vendor address file, a vendor name and number must be entered on the vendor table before this application program can be processed. Otherwise, the application program will be searching (Fig. 3.18) for a vendor number (from the PO file) that cannot be found on the vendor table.

With fixed-length records, we often discover that the cost of file design revisions may warrant alternatives like the vendor table. Oftentimes, however, we may be inheriting more data processing resources than that which meets the eye. For this application program, for example, we have acquired the following list of new data processing resources:

Vendor table (file), which must be maintained through periodic updates.

An update application program that will add or delete vendor entries in the vendor table.

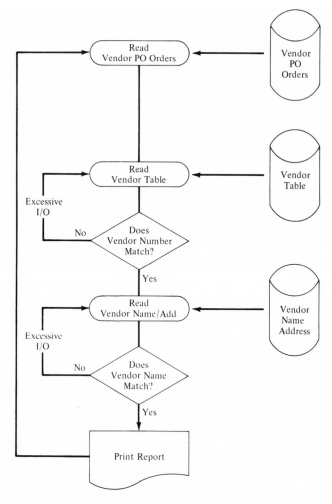

**Figure 3.18.** Excessive input/output (I/O) operations required to search files and locate search fields

A clerical task, and form design, that records the update transaction for vendor entries to be added or deleted.

The new application program that reads the PO file, vendor table, and vendor address file.

A new vendor performance file that records the vendor number, PO number, promise-to-deliver date, actual delivery date, and performance rating.*

* This new file was a result of the Purchasing Department's request to retain the vendor performance information for one year.

A creation program to build the vendor table.

Clerical efforts required to code vendor name and vendor number entries for the vendor table.

Instead of having one new application program, then, we have several application programs, clerical chores, and two new files. And the two new files may increase to at least four new files, since most installations keep backup copies.

Besides, we may have inherited less apparent problems. The application program that reads purchase orders, vendor table, and vendor address files will be using search fields to locate (and match) information from these combined files. We could encounter excessive input/output operations (Fig. 3.18) when this occurs.

As we add more files to an existing program, we may impact computer resources. For example, an operating system will schedule application programs that can execute concurrently. This, however, may depend on the number and types of files to be scheduled. If one application program uses three tape drives, the operating system will not schedule other application programs needing the same resources (see Fig. 3.19). That is, while storage can accommodate other programs, device utilization does not permit them. In other words, fewer application programs can be scheduled because device-type resources are not available.

**Figure 3.19.** Application programs that use multiple files could impact scheduling of other programs. System degradation results.

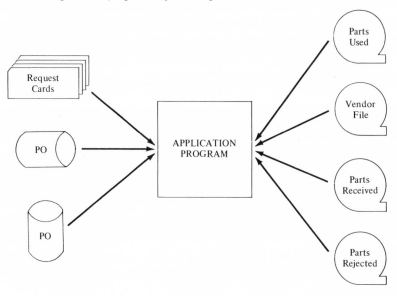

In summary, then, we can use three different formats for file design. They include fixed-length records, variable-length records, and undefined records. Since undefined records are seldom used, we have omitted them from this discussion.

When designing our files, we select the format that meets our data requirements. If our data appears fixed in length (such as a name and address file), then we would choose a fixed-length record. If our data varies in length (such as adding a new PO number to the vendor file each time a new purchase order is placed), then we would choose a variable-length record. With either file design, we can meet our data processing requirements for new applications.

When we add new application programs to an existing application area, chances are that parts (if not all) of the data elements required by the new application program already exist on our files. If parts of the data exist, then we need to revise our files to include the new data elements. With file design revisions, however, we may find ourselves in a complex data processing environment. This, of course, depends on the original file design and its implementation technique.

If we have employed the variable-length record with format-type codes for each format, then we can add the new data elements with relative simplicity. If, on the other hand, we have used the variable-length record without format-type codes, then we may be forced to revise all existing application programs that access the file in order to revise the file format. And since the same revision requirements would be needed for fixed-length records, we may find it more feasible to add new files. The new files would include the new data elements and search (or cross-reference) codes that allow the application program to merge the required files during processing. And while this technique does allow the new data processing requirement to be satisfied, it adds to the number of total data processing resources (see Fig. 3.20).

Now let's assume that most data processing installations have accumulated a large number of files, and that the number of files grew over time. Also, during the growth period, let's assume that we have all tried to add new data processing requirements to an existing system, and at one time or another have found ourselves being restricted by file design. That is, our original file design had its characteristics coded within application programs. If we revised the design, then we would be forced to revise the application programs as well. And so, we created new files in order to stabilize our existing application programs while meeting our new data processing requirements.

Having discussed the limitations encountered when revising file designs for one application program, let's measure the impact experienced when adding new application areas to our data processing system.

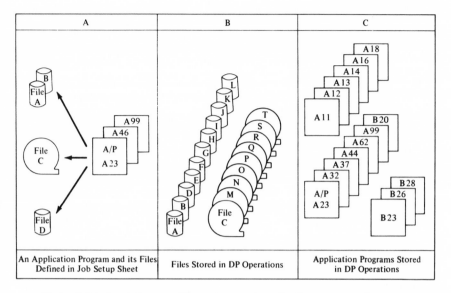

| A | B | C |
|---|---|---|
| An Application Program and its Files Defined in Job Setup Sheet | Files Stored in DP Operations | Application Programs Stored in DP Operations |

**Figure 3.20.** By adding new files and several application programs for a given requirement, data processing resources will grow astronomically over time.

## Adding a New Application Area to an Existing System

Most of our data processing systems are designed to meet the functional requirements of a given application area. For example (see Fig. 3.21) the Purchasing Department has a specific function within the organization, and therefore its purchasing system will process transactions and reports on purchasing activities. The Production Control Department assumes responsibility for monitoring production; inventory status, and order requirements. Its production control system therefore processes transactions and reports for production control activities.

Now let's assume that the production control system has been implemented, and we are in the process of adding the purchasing system. Are there any files in production control that can be used by the purchasing system? If we create new files for the purchasing system, to what extent are we duplicating our data processing resources?

Within the purchasing application area, we will find a host of complex and interrelated activities. These activities will range from placing purchase orders to monitoring the performance of vendor deliveries; from the specialization of parts

| Parts Receipt File (Production Control) | Parts Receipt File Requirements Purchasing |
|---|---|
| Part Number | PO Number |
| Part Description | Buyer Code |
| Quantity on Order | Supplier Number |
| Quantity on Hand | Part Number |
| Inspection Status | Part Description |
| Delivery Status | Quantity on Order |
| | Inspection Status |
| | Delivery Status |

**Figure 3.21.** When implementing a new system, examine an existing system's files as possible candidates for shared files.

ordered to the tracking of part replacements for rejected items. Based on these complexities, we are often forced to treat the purchasing system as a separate entity of the business during the design phase.

To design the purchasing system, we divide the function into subsets (such as new PO's, deliveries, rejects, etc.). These subsets are then analyzed for detail specifications, and the detail specifications are given to application programmers for implementation, as shown in Fig. 3.22.

At this point in the analysis, we have determined all the data element and report requirements, and we know the number of application programs required to process the purchasing system. Having designed the detail program and data element requirements, we are now ready to determine the "source" of information. Since the production control system processes the same type of data, we will examine its parts receipt file and compare its data elements to our data element requirements for a parts receipt file.

In Fig. 3.22 the production control system has a parts receipt file that contains records of each part ordered. And the purchasing system has a requirement for a parts receipt file containing the same data elements, in addition to the PO number, buyer code, and supplier number appended to the front of each record. Can the purchasing system share this file with the production control system?

If all the data elements required by an application in the purchasing system resided on this file, then the file could be shared between the two systems. Since this is not the case, we have to measure the impact of file design revisions. If the file was designed for variable-length records with format-type codes, then we can append the PO number, buyer code, and supplier number to each record and share the file. If, however, format-type codes were not used in variable-length records, or fixed-length records were employed, then the file-dependent code

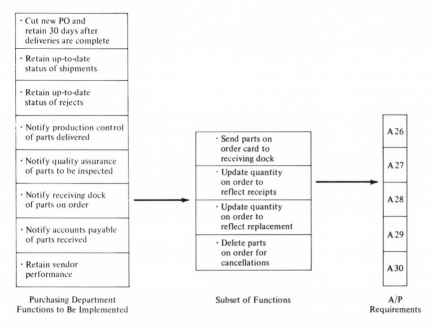

| Purchasing Department Functions to Be Implemented | Subset of Functions | A/P Requirements |

**Figure 3.22.** Dividing the functional area into subsets and application program requirements in order to implement the system

within application programs will force us to revise production control application programs if we revise their file (Fig. 3.23).

If we are meeting a deadline date for installing the purchasing system, chances are that we cannot afford the time for both file and application program revisions. Consequently, the file-dependent code in our application programs often forces us to stabilize an existing system at the expense of creating new files for our new systems. This results in duplicate data among files, duplicate update application programs, and duplicate backup files among the two systems (Fig. 3.24).

**Figure 3.23.** File-dependent code in application programs forces the revision of application programs in order to revise their file design.

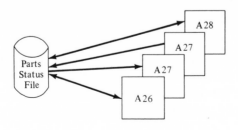

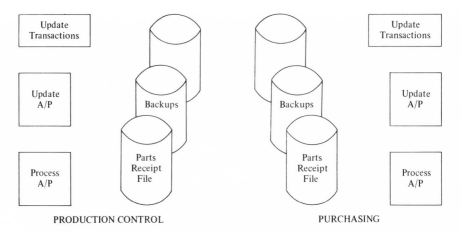

| Update Transactions | | | | Update Transactions |
| Update A/P | Backups | Backups | | Update A/P |
| Process A/P | Parts Receipt File | Parts Receipt File | | Process A/P |

PRODUCTION CONTROL                    PURCHASING

**Figure 3.24.** Although portions of data exist in one system, duplication of many resources is necessary in order to stablize A/Ps with file-dependent code.

## Inherent Problems in File Processing

Since the file-dependent code has been placed in a large percentage of our application programs, we sometimes duplicate a large percentage of our files. The end result of purchase system implementation may bring about new programmed service at the expense of duplicating a large percentage of files, their update programs, and the update transactions they process—in addition to the number of backup files required for the new files. To highlight this point, let's look at other areas of the purchasing and production control systems in which the same type of data is processed (see Fig. 3.25).

In one data processing installation, a survey was taken to determine the degree of redundant data within their systems for purchasing and accounts payable. (The results are given in Fig. 3.26.) In other words, a survey was taken on the major sort key (such as part number) and a count was taken on the number of times in which part numbers were placed in different files. In a total of 551 files, 117 files (or 21%) contained part numbers. When we view this percentage in terms of (1) duplicate update transactions, (2) duplicate update application programs, (3) duplicate scheduling of computer resources, and (4) duplicate input/output devices for backup purposes, this percentage increases astronomically.

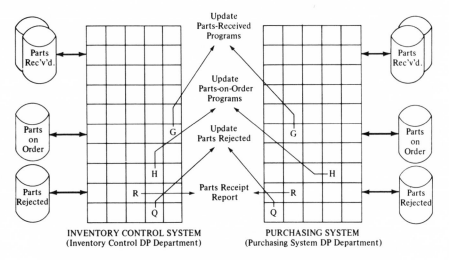

**Figure 3.25.** File-dependent code within application programs forces duplication of many areas of overlapping resources among systems.

Figure 3.27 shows the impact of backup file resources, based on the statistics I obtained from an installation.

While there are many areas to be discussed, let's summarize in a checklist the inherent data management problems that are found in most of today's installations with a large number of accumulated files.

**Figure 3.26.** Statistics reflecting the degree of redundant data stored among files designed for Purchasing and Accounts Payable Systems

| MAJOR — KEY | NO. OF FILES | % |
|---|---|---|
| PART NO. | 117 | 21 |
| DEPT. NO. | 80 | 15 |
| ACCOUNT CODE | 72 | 13 |
| DATE | 70 | 13 |
| MAN NO. | 32 | 6 |
| SUPPLIER | 15 | 3 |
| MODULE NO. | 13 | 2 |
| MACHINE NO. | 13 | 2 |
| JOB NO. | 13 | 2 |
| OTHERS | 126 | 23 |
| | 551 | 100 |

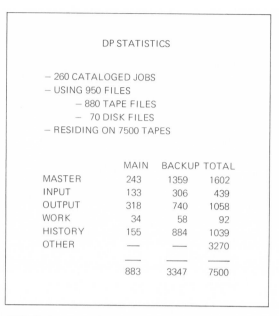

DP STATISTICS

— 260 CATALOGED JOBS
— USING 950 FILES
    — 880 TAPE FILES
    — 70 DISK FILES
— RESIDING ON 7500 TAPES

| | MAIN | BACKUP | TOTAL |
|---|---|---|---|
| MASTER | 243 | 1359 | 1602 |
| INPUT | 133 | 306 | 439 |
| OUTPUT | 318 | 740 | 1058 |
| WORK | 34 | 58 | 92 |
| HISTORY | 155 | 884 | 1039 |
| OTHER | — | — | 3270 |
| | 883 | 3347 | 7500 |

**Figure 3.27.** Data processing resources required to back up our files

## Today's Data Management Problems

The following checkpoints are grouped under files, application programs, and customer/application relationships.

**Files**

1. *Contents*
   Redundant information among records within each file (e.g., multiple Smith entries in the checking account file).

   Duplicate information among files (e.g., employee data in personnel, payroll, and medical records files).

2. *Storage Devices*
   Numerous volumes required to store data due to file design and contents.

   Increasing number of volumes (tape, disk, drum, etc.) requiring added storage space and management personnel.

3. *Design Modifications*
   Modification of existing files to accommodate new data items within a record requires:

   Re-creating the file to contain space for added data items, *and*

   Changing application programs to access modified file design, *or*

Creating new files and modifying application programs to reference those files.

4. *Maintenance*

Coordination of update activities (e.g., modifying contents of parts used, inventory, and maintenance files to delete a part).

Duplication of human effort required to submit update transactions for each file.

Reorganization of files to increase input/output performance and reuse space marked for deletion.

5. *Backup*

Excessive time required to dump file before update activities, in the event of abnormal conditions, such as:

Application program malfunction during update activities; e.g., erroneous data or ABEND condition.

Hardware malfunction on input/output device during update or retrieval activities.

Extra clerical work required to store and maintain backup files accumulated from update activities.

6. *Recovery*

Manpower time required to document recovery procedures for each file. CPU time required to rerun all update programs which executed during interim period.

7. *Single File Access*

System/360 and System/370 performance impact when using sequential access to "selected" records.

Excessive input/output operations required to bypass undesired records. Impact on system execution due to channel (S/370) or device (S/360) contention.

File sort overhead to obtain data in a different sort sequence.

Program modification overhead to improve performance through device or access method changes.

8. *Multiple File Access*

"Await Resource Availability" occurrence if scheduling multiple file programs in a multiprocessing system:

Device type availability (tape unit, disk pack, etc.).

Data set availability since "exclusive usage" occurs in update processing mode.

Locate, mount, and dismount activities often required by machine operators.

Excessive CPU and input/output required to search cross-referenced files.

Impact expressed under "7. Single File Access" compounded when sequentially referencing several files.

## Application Programs

1. *Design*
   Heavily dependent upon file designs and their interrelationships (cross-reference interdependencies).

   Excessive time dedicated to programming and debugging input/output logic of single or multiple file access.

   Extensive experience required to understand file declarations within application program.

   Documentation of operating procedures for application program and backup/reorganization procedures for each file.

2. *Maintenance*
   To modify program, considerable effort initially required to study input/output logic.

   Impact can become so time-consuming and tedious that customer's request is often denied on basis of cost.

   Industry momentarily crippled by program staff changes. (Loss of application maintenance analyst could result in extensive "replacement" training due to file/program complexities.)

   Modification of program documentation and file maintenance procedures (if access method changed).

## Customer/Application Relationship

1. *Report Contents*
   Sequentially processed data may cause large reports, with desired information embedded within.

   Most recent data may not reside on all files containing duplicate information, causing a discrepancy among printed reports.

2. *Delayed Reactions*
   Request for program modifications may generate large time estimates due to file/program interdependencies.

3. *Increased Costs*
   Performance improvement and/or service expansion usually results in additional equipment, and/or manpower (e.g., larger computers, program or file design modifications, or operating procedure changes like RJE, HASP, etc., to improve throughout).

# 4 Data Base Design Environment

Within the "File Design Environment" (Chap. 3) we have discussed file design and the restrictions encountered when attempting to revise designs by adding new requirements to our data processing systems. We have identified the restrictions as being the file-dependent code within our application programs. And to stabilize our existing system, we have often been forced to add new files with each new data element requirement. With the new files came a host of inherent file management problems, as we pointed out at the conclusion of Chapter 3.

Many of the inherent problems in file design can be resolved with a good data base system. Let's define the term "good data base system" by saying we need a system that allows us to (1) revise the design of data without revising our application programs, (2) share our data among application areas without exposing confidential items to unauthorized users, and (3) back up our files in less input/output volumes than typically used in a file-design environment.

Many of today's data base products meet these objectives. Unfortunately, many of today's software products use the same terminology (such as data independence and data security) for degrees of feature implementation. That is, data independence in one program product will differ from data independence in another program product. With this in mind, I have defined the best of each feature, and have shown limitations where I know them to exist. By doing so, I know the reader will be equipped with the necessary background to obtain the details of specific program products from his local salesman.

With this in mind, we will approach the "Data Base Design Environment" in terms of the features it provides that resolve many of the data management problems that can be found in a file design environment. In other words, let's assume that we have a data processing installation that contains a large number of files to support the programmed services for each application area. And let's assume that we want to resolve the inherent problems in file design with the features contained in a good data base system. What are these features, and what are their cost-savings areas?

## Storage Reduction

To reduce our storage requirements, we need a data base system that stores data hierarchically. That is, we want to store an item only once, even though there are multiple entries for that item. To highlight this point, let's use the banking industry to contrast the difference between the fixed-length record and the hierarchical record (see Fig. 4.1).

As you can see, there are four record entries for one customer's deposit activities. Each record contains the customer's name and account number. In other words, these items are repeated each time a deposit is made. To reduce store, we can store one copy of the customer's name and account number, using a hierarchical structure.

To employ a hierarchical structure, we need to examine the relationship between data elements (items) within the four records. We find two relationships existing: a one-to-one and a one-to-many. Now, a one-to-one relationship occurs when data elements share a unique (one-to-one) relationship with each other. A typical example would include the items given in Fig. 4.2. In other words, an individual can have only one Social Security number (SS No.), sex, age and marital status: We say that a one-to-one relationship exists between the customer name and his SS number, sex, age, and marital status descriptors. A one-to-

**Figure 4.1.** In a banking environment fixed-length records containing one file entry per banking activity are found.

| Customer Name | Account Number | Date of Deposit | Amount Deposited |
|---|---|---|---|
| Marini, Ronald J. | 11-141-2320 | 12-15-75 | $450.00 |
| Marini, Ronald J. | 11-141-2320 | 12-25-75 | $450.00 |
| Marion, James | 11-168-2745 | 12-13-75 | $275.00 |
| Marion, James | 11-168-2748 | 12-20-75 | $275.00 |

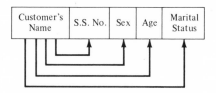

**Figure 4.2.** For each Customer Name, there can only be one SS#, Sex, Age and Marital Status.

many relationship exists between the customer name and deposit information (date of deposit and amount deposited) because a customer can have one or more deposit activities.

To use a hierarchical structure, we need to cluster our one-to-one data elements into one record entry. In Fig. 4.3 we have grouped checking account items into two types of entries: (1) a customer entry (containing customer name and account number); and (2) a deposit entry (containing deposit date and deposit amount). *The one-to-many relationship does not exist within either entry.* Instead, the one-to-many relationship refers to the implied relationship between the customer entry and the deposit entry. That is, for each customer entry, we can have one or more deposit entries appended.

Now, does this reduce storage? Thus far we have only illustrated the case where a customer has made *one* deposit. Let's extend this illustration in Fig. 4.4 by including another deposit. As you can see, we have just reduced storage by 50% among the two checking account records for Ronald J. Marini. Instead of repeating customer name and account number, we simply append the new deposit information to the end of the last-recorded entry. Savings increase as we append more deposit entries for this customer. By reducing storage requirements, we reduce I/O (input/output) devices, device mounting, operator intervention, and scheduling delays.

When acquiring a data base system, be sure it has the capability to store data

**Figure 4.3.** Using the records displayed previously, divide the data elements by grouping them into record entries. Each entry must contain those data elements that share a one-to-one relationship.

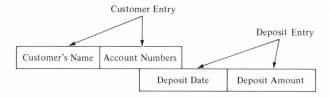

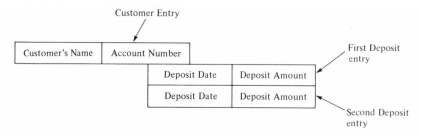

**Figure 4.4.** As new deposits are made, simply append the deposit entries to the end without repeating information within the customer entry.

in this manner. If *storage reductions* are not within the system, you may be carrying your old files (and their problems) into a new environment. Should this occur, you'll be in more trouble farther down the road. Indeed, you've postponed storage efficiency at the expense of conversion efforts for a temporary cure.

Should you choose a data base system with the *storage reduction* feature, you will have to convert existing files into a new format. You need not convert all files at once, however. Your planner can schedule conversion effort on a "phase" plan. Since there are other cost savings in interrelated features, let's just summarize the *storage reduction* feature at this time.

### Cost Savings of the Storage Reduction Feature

Storage reduction gives us four distinct advantages:

*I/O Device Reduction:* By storing record entries in segments, you can add new segments to the end of an existing entry.

By reducing storage for a single file, you are freeing up space on the device. That space can be shared with other files.

*Device Mount Reduction:* By storing more files on a device, you can keep the most frequently used files mounted.

*Operator Intervention Reduction:* When application programs access files that are already mounted, the operators need not locate and mount devices.

*Program Scheduling Delays Reduced:* If all resources are available, the operating system need not delay scheduling of an application program.

## File Consolidation

Most data base (DB) systems provide file consolidation as an extension to the storage reduction feature. To consolidate files, we start with a single file layout and divide items into unique entry types. That is, we group the one-to-one

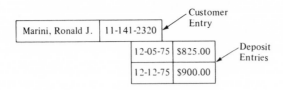

**Figure 4.5.**

items into a unique entry type (just like the customer entry). Since deposits can vary in number, we group its information into another entry type (just like the deposit entry). Recall that the one-to-many relationship implies multiple occurrences of the deposit entry for a given occurrence of the customer entry.

Also recall that we reduced storage by segmenting (dividing) the total information into unique entry types. That is, we share a single copy of the customer name and account number with multiple deposit entries (Fig. 4.5). We can also share a single copy of the customer entry with other types of entries when we consolidate files. To do this, we must examine other files that contain the *same type of information*. This is illustrated in Fig. 4.6.

Let's examine the format of the checking account (withdrawal) file and review some record entries for Ronald J. Marini (Fig. 4.7). To merge these record entries into our new deposit file, we must first examine each item for one-to-one and one-to-many relationships. Again we find a one-to-one relationship between customer name and account number. Since a customer can have multiple deposits, we are forced to place deposit information into another entry type such as that in Fig. 4.8.

Now that we've defined relationships and segmented the original record entries, we can merge the withdrawal file into the deposit file. By merging these two files, we have reduced storage as well as the number of input/output devices accessed by the application program. Instead of accessing daily deposit and with-

**Figure 4.6.** In a banking environment the above files all contain the Customer's Name and Account Number information

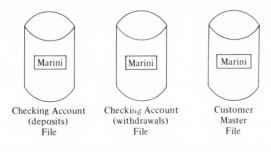

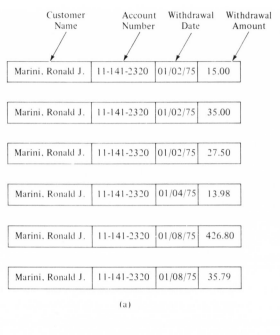

(a)

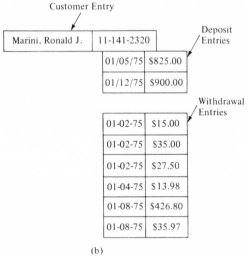

(b)

**Figure 4.7.** By consolidating Deposit and Withdrawal Files (a) we can share a single copy of Customer information with multiple Deposit and Withdrawal entries (b).

Customer Entry
Withdrawal Entries
Marini, Ronald J.
11-141-2320
01/02/75 15.00
01/02/75 35.00
01/02/75 27.50
01/04/75 13.98
01/08/75 426.80
01/08/75 35.97

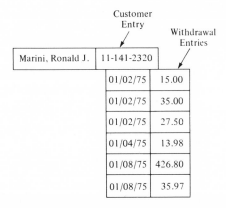

**Figure 4.8.** While examining the Deposit File for one-to-one relationships, two unique categories (types) of information were found: Customer and Deposit.

drawal information from two different files, the application program needs only to access the consolidated file.

Let's see if we can achieve further reductions by examining the customer master file in Fig. 4.9, where all items have a one-to-one relationship with each other. That is, Ronald J. Marini has one checking account number, resident address, employer and address, resident telephone, sex, marital status, birthdate, Social Security number, account balance, and average monthly balance. With this in mind, let's add the record entry of Fig. 4.10 to our new file.

Now our customer entry contains the customer name, account number, and all the items illustrated in Fig. 4.9 (represented by the ellipse dots in Fig. 4.10). Again we have reduced storage (1) by storing a single copy of the customer's information, and (2) by sharing that information with the deposit and withdrawal entries. We have consolidated files by merging the information into a hierarchi-

**Figure 4.9.** A record entry for Ronald J. Marini extracted from the Checking Account Master File

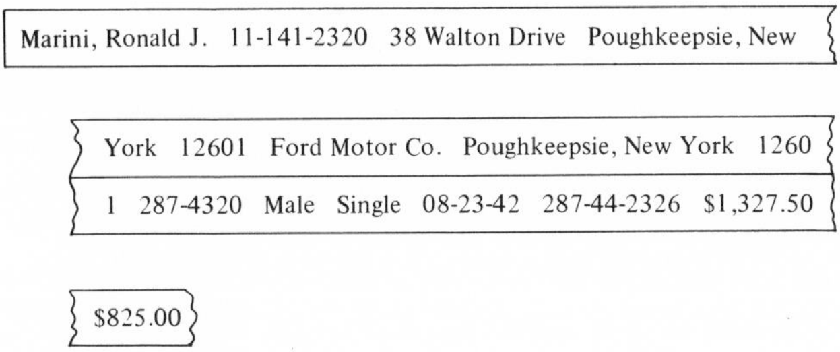

Marini, Ronald J. 11-141-2320 38 Walton Drive Poughkeepsie, New
York 12601 Ford Motor Co. Poughkeepsie, New York 1260
1 287-4320 Male Single 08-23-42 287-44-2326 $1,327.50
$825.00

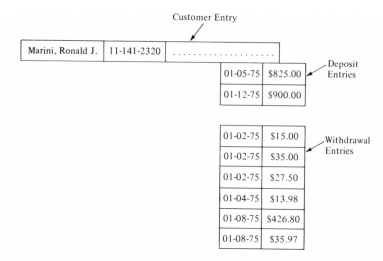

**Figure 4.10.** In our consolidated file (data base), we have the Customer Entry (from Customer Master, Deposit and Withdrawal Files) as well as Deposit and Withdrawal Entries.

cal structure (Fig. 4.11). That is, we grouped items according to their one-to-one relationship, thereby segmenting the information into unique entry (segment) types. By doing so, we have designed a data base. *A data base can be defined as a collection of files that contain common data elements, such as customer name, which are reformatted according to one-to-one and one-to-many relationships.*

Now let's see how this has improved our operating environment. Again we have reduced the number of files and thereby reduced file access and device allocation, as Fig. 4.11 illustrates.

We can take file consolidation into other application areas. Before we do that, let's ask what files should be consolidated. *If files contain "common data elements" (items), they can be merged into a "common data base."* For example, we know that deposits, withdrawals, and checking account master files contained common (duplicate) items. That is, each contained the customer's name and account number. We also know that *each of these files* contained information that related to the same customer. We call these duplicated items "common data elements." By combining files into a "common" data base, we are consolidating files, reducing storage, and reducing program logic. Thus far, however, we've only consolidated files in one application area. Let's consolidate files among other application areas before discussing advantages.

If we examine the personal loan application area, we find a large percentage of duplicate (common) items. That is, we find the majority of customers had

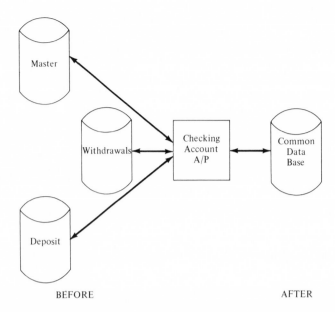

BEFORE                                             AFTER

**Figure 4.11.** Merging files with "common" information into data base gives a better operating environment.

checking accounts and personal loans in the same bank. Now, the personal loan master file contains some of the same personal items as the data base. We find customer name, address, employer, Social Security, etc. We can easily let the data base segment for checking accounts represent the personal loan segment. We do have one problem, however. When we looked at data element relationships for checking accounts, we found a one-to-one relationship between customer name and account number. If we "share" this segment with the personal loans application area, we have to change the relationship. Thus, Ronald J. Marini will have a checking account number and also a personal loan number. We would therefore restructure the customer segment as shown in Fig. 4.12.

**Figure 4.12.** The merger of the Personal Loans File into data base requires removal of account-type items from the Customer Entry.

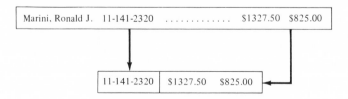

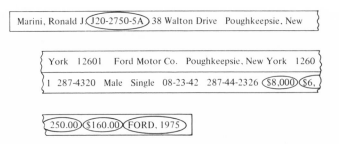

**Figure 4.13.** Information stored for Ronald J. Marini within the Personal Loan Master File

After removing account-related information (e.g., account number, account balance, and average monthly balance) from the customer segment, we can examine the personal loan master file (Fig. 4.13). As you can see, most of the information in the personal loan master file has already been placed in the customer segment. The circled items in Fig. 4.13 denote those fields that do not appear in our data base. If we examine the circled fields, we find that J20-2750-5A is the account number, $8,000 is the loan amount, $6,250 is the loan balance, $160.00 is the monthly payment, and FORD 1975 is the purchased item. Since all the circled fields describe the type of loan, and since they have a one-to-one relationship with each other, we can place them in the same segment type, as indicated in Fig. 4.14. Since we have created only one new segment type, let's proceed by merging this new segment into our data base (Fig. 4.15).

We have examined the records in the personal loan master file and have found that most of the information had already been placed in the customer segment. Since we have two account types (or a one-to-many relationship between the customer name and the number of accounts he may have), we reformatted (Fig. 4.15) the customer segment A and created a new checking account segment B. We also created a personal loan segment C, containing the account number, loan amount, loan balance, monthly payment amount, and purchased item.

Within the Personal Loan Department, we have another file that records monthly payments as they are made. The monthly payment file contains the cus-

**Figure 4.14.** When merging the Personal Loan Master File into data base, account-type information must be placed in a unique segment.

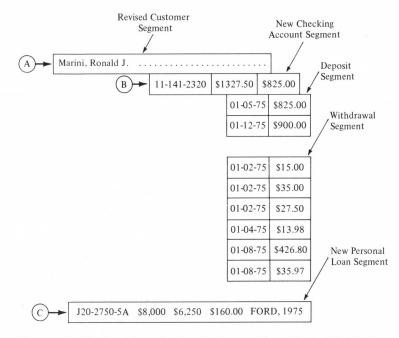

**Figure 4.15.** Merging information from the Personal Loan Master File into data base

tomer loan, account number, payment date, and amount-paid information (Fig. 4.16). As you can see, we have already stored the customer name in the customer segment, and we have already stored the account number in the personal loan segment. To merge this file into our data base, we need only add a payment segment.

To this point, we've merged five files into a "shared" data base. We say it is shared because it can be accessed by two or more application areas. In other words, this data base satisfies the needs of checking account and personal loan application areas. We can extend this data base to include other application areas

**Figure 4.16.** The Monthly Payment File used to store payment information for each monthly payment.

| Customer Name | Account Number | Payment Date | Payment Amount |
|---|---|---|---|
| Marini, Ronald J. | J20-2750-5A | 01-15-75 | $160.00 |
| Marini, Ronald J. | J20-2750-5A | 02-15-75 | $320.00 |

by analyzing their data and merging entries just as we've done for these files. Candidates would include mortgage, savings, and charge card application areas.

By consolidating our files into a "shared" data base, we reduce storage within a single file (storing segments) and among files containing common (duplicate) data elements. We can also reduce computer utilization and program logic within the programmer's code. Let's look more closely at these data processing enhancements.

You will recall that the Checking Account Department had three major files: daily deposits, daily withdrawals, and a master file. To generate the monthly statements, an application program would read these files, compare names and account numbers, and merge information from these files into a single report. Using the data base approach, the files have already been merged. The application program need only access the segments and generate the monthly statement. In other words, file searches and record merging can be removed from application code, thereby reducing program logic.

File consolidation allows us to "share" a single copy of data with other application areas. By doing this, we *improve data integrity*. Now let's look at this enhancement relative to customer satisfaction. Remember the student whose tuition-due notice was lost in the mail after he had completed the change-of-address card. This was due to the number of files containing his name and address (Fig. 4.17). And while his file had been updated for the Department of Registration, update activities had not been applied to the other files. Consider how this situation can be avoided.

If these files are merged into a common data base, we can share a single copy of the student's personal data in a segment. We can then share this segment with all application areas (excluding honor roll). When we change the student's address, the most recent data becomes available to all application areas. Let's compare the difference in operating procedures. Figure 4.18 shows the updating of the file design environment; Fig. 4.19, of the data base environment (and data

**Figure 4.17.** In a university environment many files contain the student's name and address

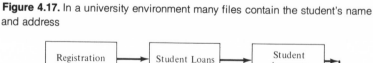
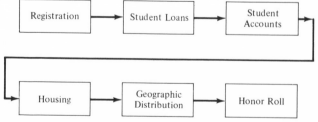

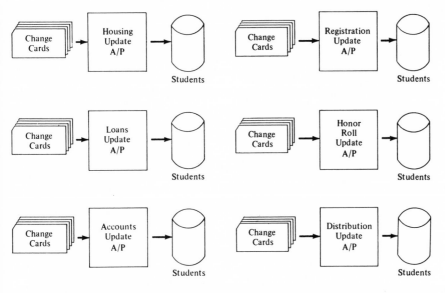

**Figure 4.18.** In a standard file design environment, update (change) cards in each area that must revise its files have to be prepared.

**Figure 4.19.** In a data base environment change the student's address only once: the revised segment becomes available immediately to all applications.

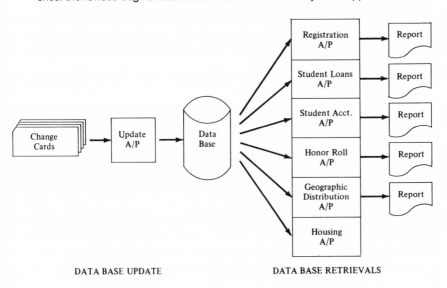

DATA BASE UPDATE                    DATA BASE RETRIEVALS

57

base update and retrievals). Thus, as opposed to executing update programs in each application area (with intervening clerical chores and elapsed time), we can update a single copy of the student's personal data. In other words, we improve data integrity for all application users while reducing update processing, clerical chores, and files.

While there are other enhancements in file consolidation, these enhancements introduce other data base features that we haven't discussed. To summarize: By *file consolidation* we receive all the enhancements listed as cost savings in the preceding section (Storage Reduction), plus those listed below.

### Cost Savings in File Consolidation

We see now that we have gained five additional advantages as follows:

*Storage Reduction:* When files are merged, we can store a single copy of previously duplicated items.

*Program Logic Reductions:* Since the required information is stored in a shared data base, we can eliminate multiple file access and search routines within the application program.

*Improved Data Integrity:* If we store a single copy of data and share it among application areas, the most recent copy becomes available to all users at the same time.

*Clerical Task Reduction:* By retaining one source of shared information, we reduce the clerical tasks required in other application areas.

*Program Execution Reduction:* By retaining one source of shared information, we eliminate the need to execute update programs within each application area.

## Data Independence

Many data base systems offer varying degrees of data independence. If you recall, data independence was defined as the installation's ability to add new items (data elements) to an existing file without changing the "old" application programs. In this section we'll discuss data independence as it relates to "shared" data bases. I'll denote data base shortcomings where appropriate.

In the past, we displayed all the segment types by showing each occurrence (entry). That is, we showed two Deposit Segments if two deposits were made. Instead of illustrating all the entries, let's assign symbolic names to our segment types: The symbolic names and the data they represent are defined in Fig. 4.20. Just as we draw a hierarchical structure for corporate organizations, we can place these segments in a data base hierarchy (see Fig. 4.21).

| | |
|---|---|
| CUSTOMER | Personal data segment, containing the customer's name and other personal information |
| CHECKING | Checking account segment, containing the account number, account balance, and average monthly balance. |
| DEPOSIT | Daily deposit segment, containing the deposit date and amount deposited. |
| WITHDRAW | Daily withdrawal segment, containing the date cashed and the check amount. |
| LOANS | Personal loan segment, containing the loan number and terms. |
| PAYMENTS | Monthly payment segment, containing the payment date and amount. |

**Figure 4.20.**

In some data base systems, the loan application program would access customer checking, deposit, and withdraw in order to access loans and payments. In other data base systems, the loan application program can access customer, loans and payments, while bypassing access of segments that it does not need to process. In the latter case, we say that the application program has *data independence*. That is, the application program need not know the format of nonprocessed segments.

Now suppose that the financial statement program generated a report on current loans and their balances. This application program would need to access the customers and loans segments. If data independence is provided on the *segment level,* then this application program can bypass accessing the payments segment. Again we say that this provides data independence because the application program need not access segments that aren't processed. Thus, it need not be famil-

**Figure 4.21.** A hierarchical representation of the types of segments defined in the Customer Master Data Base

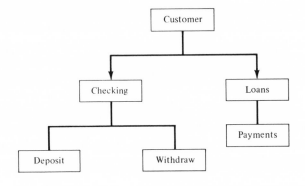

**Figure 4.22.** By using specific segment types, the application program can view this data as only containing its segments (or subset of the total structure).

iar with the formats of nonprocessed segments. To the loan application program, the data base would appear as in Fig. 4.22.

Stated differently, loan programs need not know about segments used by checking account programs. We therefore have two application areas that "share" customer segments without superimposing the need to access all segment types in the data base. With this definition in mind, let's go back to our earlier definition of data independence.

Can we add new field(s) to the end of a segment without changing "old" application programs that don't need to reference the new field(s)? Before viewing this, let's ask, "How important is this capability?" First of all, data bases allow us to "share" file-type resources among application areas. To do this, we need to consolidate files that have common (duplicate) fields. Now, chances are that our files are numerous—and application processing is rather intricate. Therefore, it would not be feasible to convert all application areas at the same time. We'd have to convert one application area (e.g., checking accounts) before converting another application area (e.g., personal loans). When we convert the second application area, we may find fields that should be added to an existing segment. Personal loans, for example, may retain the customer's employment data (such as salary) that is not required by the Checking Account Department. We would therefore want to add salary to the customer segment. In other words, we have a very practical application for this capability in data bases, although some data base systems allow us this degree of data independence at the expense of a few installation headaches.

To add new items to an existing segment, installations would have to employ the *variable-length feature*. Variable length means that a segment can vary in size. While it was intended for other applications, variable length can be used for segment growth. Let's see how this would happen.

First, you'd define a segment as a variable-length segment. Then you'd reserve a four-byte count field (Fig. 4.23). This field then tells the length of the segment.

If subsequent fields were added to the end of the customer segment, you'd

Appended COUNT field     Customer segment

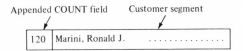

| 120 | Marini, Ronald J. | . . . . . . . . . . . . . . |

**Figure 4.23.** By reserving the COUNT field, new fields (items) can be added to the end.

simply change the count field and add new item(s). This is quite feasible because it allows the segment to grow without impacting existing application programs. Unfortunately, the count field is stored on disk, causing storage requirements to increase by four bytes per customer. This storage overhead could be avoided if data base systems allowed a segment type to increase its size without using variable length. In other words, the data base system should allow a segment to change (e.g., from 120 to 135) without using a count field. We're assuming, of course, that all customer entries should include the new fields. If that is not the case, variable length will not accommodate your needs. That is, loan customers will have their salaries recorded while nonloan customers will not.

The intended usage of the variable-length segment feature was aimed at segments that vary in length. That is, some customers may be married while others are not. Married customers may have their names appended to the end of a segment, whereas single customers would not (Fig. 4.24). In other words, the variable-length segment feature allows us to reduce segments to 120 bytes for single customers. We avoid wasting 15 bytes of storage per single customer. Again, this feature helps us use storage efficiently for varying fields. It *can* be employed to allow segments to change their size as we add new application requirements. I do not recommend this as an ultimate solution. That, of course, remains in the hands of customers and their software companies.

Another form of data independence can be obtained from data base systems that remove I/O (input/output) attributes from the application program. Let's look momentarily at some of these "coded" attributes (Fig. 4.25).

Should you change these attributes, the probability is that you will have to change all application programs that reference this file. As stated earlier, this

**Figure 4.24.** Using the Variable-Length-Segment feature to include the spouse's name for married customers. Decrease COUNT to 120 for single customers.

Count          Customer                 Wife

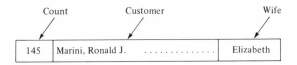

| 145 | Marini, Ronald J. | . . . . . . . . . . . . . | Elizabeth |

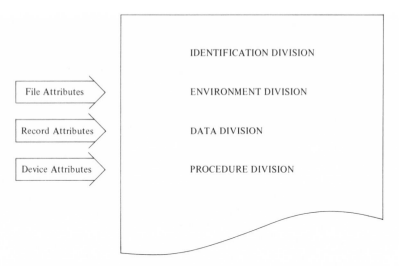

**Figure 4.25.** A COBOL application program containing degrees of file, record, and device attributes within the code

becomes quite a bottleneck because (1) programs using this file are not always identifiable, (2) application programs may not be properly documented, and (3) application programmers who write the code are not always accessible. In some cases, files become stagnant and obsolete. In other cases, computer performance can be crippled by poor access methods that require excessive I/O (input/output) activities.

Good data base systems will provide a data management system between the application program and the data base (Fig. 4.26). In this way, the application calls the data base system for input/output (I/O) services instead of coding these services within the application program.

As you can see in Fig. 4.26, the data base attributes have been removed from the application program (A/P). Using this approach, you can change device types (e.g., convert from 2314 to 3330 device types), access methods (e.g., convert from sequential to direct access), or record size without changing your application programs (Fig. 4.27). This allows upward migration in hardware without the cost of installation conversion efforts. This form of data independence also reduces application coding.

Another cost-savings factor would include computer performance. Since an application program is assigned to a specific programmer, that employee becomes responsible for all program resources, which includes file design. Since the programmer isn't trained for hardware performance considerations, file design could result in average system degradation. This problem is not always

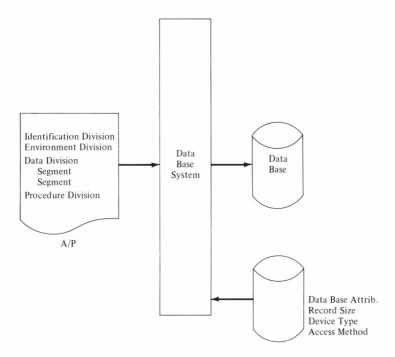

**Figure 4.26.** In a data base environment describe only those segments that will be processed within the application program.

recognizable. We simply know that program A has an execution time of 45 minutes and we bill the user accordingly.

Using a data base system (with this form of data independence), we are merging many files, reducing storage requirements, and sharing resources among application areas. The scope of a data base can become so significant that we can easily cost-justify an expert in data base design. This expert (often called the

**Figure 4.27.** Using a data base system to change access methods, device types, etc., without changing each application program

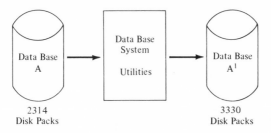

Data Base Administrator, or DBA) can examine the processing requirements and design for performance. This offers a twofold advantage. It removes file design from application programmer responsibilities while enhancing computer performance through DBA expertise.

This offers greater room for future enhancements as our processing requirements change. For example, we may find ourselves designing for performance in July 1975. As time progresses, our volume of data may change, creating the need to reevaluate our data base system. Performance studies may indicate the need to change access methods. This open-ended approach to data base management allows us to change with the times with relative simplicity.

While other views of data independence can be stated, let's examine these in later sections (Evolutionary Growth and Programmer Productivity).

### Cost Savings Areas of Data Independence

Four distinct advantages are outcomes of data independence, as follows:

*Programming Flexibility:* By referencing symbolic segment names, application programs need not access those segments that are not processed. By bypassing nonprocessed segment types, application programmers need not be aware of segments belonging to other application areas.

*Segment Growth Potential:* By using the variable-length segment feature, a segment can change in size without revising application programs that do not need to access the new fields.

*Changing Data Base Attributes:* If installations change device types, access methods, etc., to enhance performance, these data base changes do not impact existing application programs.

*Enhanced Computer Performance:* If new input/output (I/O) devices are introduced, installation can change data base devices without changing application programs.

If one employee is assigned data base design responsibilities (e.g., data base administration), input/output performance can be improved through the efficient design of a "shared" resource.

## Data Base Security

When we consider merging files, we'd like to consolidate resources without the loss of privacy for each application area. This precaution is called "data base security" (Fig. 4.28). Good data base systems will offer some form of security for their users. This may range from passwords coded within the application pro-

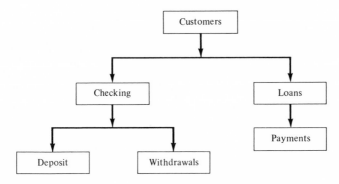

**Figure 4.28.** Using the bank's data base to highlight the features within data base security

gram to "operator" approval for a job to be executed. The highest form of data base security requires "segment level" containment.

*Segment level security* functions in several ways. First of all, installations define a security control block for *each application program,* which would contain the following information:

```
Application program name
   Data base name 1
      .
      .
      .

      Segment access 1
         Usage authorized 1
         Usage authorized 2
         .
         .
         .

      Segment access N
         .
         .
         .
         .
         .

   Data base name N
      .
      .
      .
```

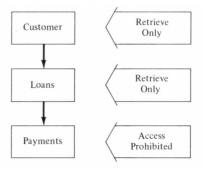

**Figure 4.29.** Using segment level security to control the type of processing that can be performed on each segment type

Now the application program name would be a unique name assigned to an application program. For each data base to be accessed, the Data Base Administrator would specify the data base name and segments that can be accessed. Data base security also allows the Data Base Administrator to limit the type of processing that can be performed on a given segment type. See Fig. 4.29.

For example, the loan application program can be limited to retrieval-only activities for customers and loans.

    Program Name:   Loans report  
        Data Base:   Customer master  
         Segment:   Name = Customers  
                     Access = Retrieve only  
         Segment:   Name = Loans  
                     Access = Retrieve only

Thus, segment level security prevents this application program from accessing segments other than the customers and loans segments. It further prevents this application program from changing fields within the customers and loans segments. In other words, the application program can retrieve only these segments. Update activities are prohibited. See Fig. 4.30.

You may ask whether the application programmer can change his processing security. That would depend upon security procedures at your installation. If the data base system stored your program's security control blocks in a unique library, the library can be conorolled by the DP operations staff. One installation I visited has protected this library by using an operator request to update its contents. The operator reviews a sign-off control form that must be submitted by the Data Base Administrator. If the form is intact, the operator allows the change to occur. Otherwise, the job is canceled.

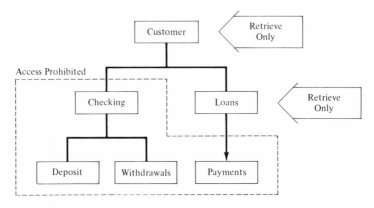

**Figure 4.30.** The Loan Application Program can only retrieve Customer and Loans segments using data base security.

Some installations want stringent security controls, while others operate quite casually. For those desirous of "tight" security, there is one factor worthy of mention. For most data base systems, security occurs on the segment level (Fig. 4.31), not the field level. In other words, we can protect the segment in several ways (lock out access or limit access to retrieval only). If an application programmer is authorized to update a segment, however, he can revise any field within the segment type.

The loans payment program, for example, can be authorized to insert

**Figure 4.31.** Using segment level security to control the type of processing that can be performed on each segment type

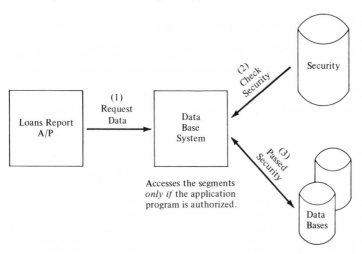

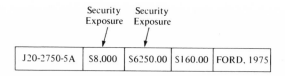

**Figure 4.32.** An application program authorized to update the Loans segment can change any field within that segment. A security exposure may occur if invalid changes are made, such as changing Loan Amount from $8,000 to $6,000.

monthly payments and revise the balance due. This program could change the loan amount and loan balance, since both fields are within the same segment (Fig. 4.32). We are then presented with the problem of preventing an application program from updating unauthorized fields within a segment. An approach to this field-level security would be to use the one-to-one relationship to design segments, excluding security-exposure fields. We could thus place the security-exposure fields in a separate segment type (Fig. 4.33).

With field-level security, we pay the price in larger software packages and increased execution time, since our data base system would check security for each program access. With segment-level security, we can "lock" secure fields by dividing a segment (e.g., loans or loan amounts), as shown in Fig. 4.34. When examining segments for possible subdivision, we should review only "shared" segments. That is, we should examine segments that are processed by two or more application areas (e.g., customers). The loans segment is probably exclusively owned. That is, the Checking Account Department is probably the only department that has application programs accessing LOANS and PAYMENTS. While the loans segment can be divided for security purposes, I would probably leave this decision in the hands of the checking account application area.

**Figure 4.33.** Dividing a segment into one or more segments to protect field(s) against unauthorized changes. In this case the Loan Amount segment (containing only the Loan Amount Field) can be protected.

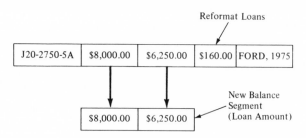

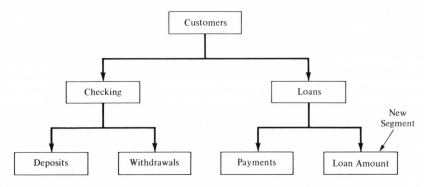

**Figure 4.34.** Illustrating the location of our new Loan Amount segment containing security exposure fields (Loan Amount and Loan Balance)

In summary, data base security is a means of protecting segments in a "shared" data base environment.

### Data Base Security Enhancements

Data base security results in two important enhancements as follows:

*Segment-Level Control:* Enhancement here has a dual effect.

By storing security control blocks that authorize programs to update or retrieve a given segment, we receive greater security than exists in today's files.

By authorizing application programs to access specific segments, we can consolidate files without losing "ownership" privileges among application areas (e.g., loans and payments belong to the Loans Department).

*Program Consolidation Potential:* For shared segments, we could pool update requirements into one update program per "shared" segment. As a result, we'd improve data security for those segments.

## Evolutionary Growth

When we discuss "evolutionary growth," we're referring to the ability to add new applications to an existing system. We may want to add new programmed services or we may want to merge new applications into the existing system. We'll discuss both capabilities in this section.

Evolutionary growth usually refers to our ability *to add new applications to the system.* In the banking environment, for example, we could add mortgages

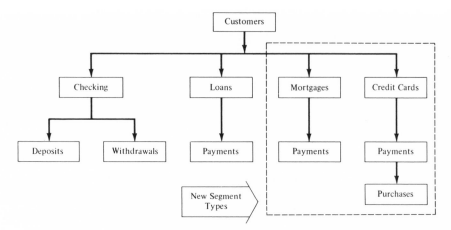

**Figure 4.35.** With evolutionary growth, new segment types can be added without revising existing application programs.

and credit card applications to the existing data base structure (Fig. 4.35). The new segment types would not impact existing application programs; that is, we could add new segment types without revising the application programs that access the ''old'' segment types.

With the variable-length segment feature, we can extend evolutionary growth to include segment format changes. Suppose, for example, we designed the customers segment by collecting data elements from the checking account and loans application areas. When we analyzed requirements for the mortgage application area, we found the need to store the spouse's name, employer, employer address, and salary. We can revise the customers segment format, as in Fig. 4.36, to include these new data elements, using the variable-length segment feature.

In other words, we can add new fields to the end of a segment without revising application programs. Since we store these new fields only for customers

**Figure 4.36.** Using the Variable-Length-Segment feature to revise the Customers segment format

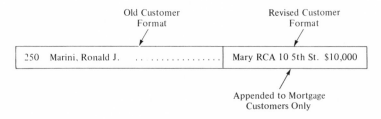

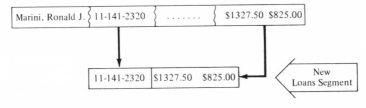

**Figure 4.37.** Splitting the Customers segment to accommodate the Personal Loans application

with mortgage accounts, we reduce storage for segment entries of customers that do not have mortgages. Therefore, we need not reserve space for the new fields (such as new loans in Fig. 4.37) in nonmortgage entries.

There are severe problems encountered when we change a segment format in other ways. Suppose, for example, we had defined the customers segment as a fixed length. If we were to change it to variable length and add the count field, we would have to revise application programs to (1) include the count field description in the segment description area, and (2) examine the count field when processing the segment. This "after-the-fact" change causes revisions in existing application programs. To avoid this, we could define "shared" segments as variable-length segments during the design phase.

Another problem occurs when we examine one-to-one relationships within one application area and design accordingly. You will recall that we designed the data base for the checking account area initially. When we added the personal loans area, we discovered a one-to-many relationship between the customer name and account number. We reformatted the customers segment and placed account information in a unique segment type.

If we had already implemented checking account application programs, these programs would need revisions. To avoid this, we need to plan for short-range and long-range applications. Afterward, we can design for one application area. Upon completion, we need to sign off other application areas. That is, we let other application areas examine the data elements, indicating their usage. With this information, you can revise the data base design and proceed with implementation.

In view of complex data base systems (such as purchasing and general ledger) sign-off procedures may not guarantee against segment splitting.

When designing a data base we must start with a single function. This allows us to analyze data processing requirements by first examining existing files. In the purchasing system, for example, you may find the statistics (gathered from a DP installation) listed in Fig. 4.38.

```
–260 CATALOGUED JOBS
–USING 950 FILES
      –880 TAPE FILES
      – 70 DISK FILES
–RESIDING ON 7500 TAPES

                    MAIN         BACKUP        TOTAL
    MASTER          243          1359          1602
    INPUT           133          306           439
    OUTPUT          318          740           1058
    WORK            34           58            92
    HISTORY         155          884           1039
    OTHER           —            —             3270
                    ───          ────          ────
                    883          3347          7500
```

**Figure 4.38.** Existing file in Purchasing System

As you can see, data base design for a single application (function) requires massive efforts. We cannot possibly design for all applications simultaneously. To avoid revisions within application programs for each revision in data base design, we should use variable-length segments. In this way, a new application will have a minimal impact on our system.

Let's just say that our best data base packages provide for evolutionary growth. This growth, however, should be described as "permissible" changes that do not impact our existing system. Graphically, we can display permissible changes as shown in Fig. 4.39.

*To add new programmed services,* we simply revise or add application programs. If we revise an existing application program, we still encounter the traditional problem associated with changing another programmer's code—if the original programmer isn't available. However, we're more organized for changes. First of all, we're accessing a "shared" data base. By sharing "common" data, we have generated in-house standards for field lengths, naming conventions, etc. When did this happen?

When we force ourselves to examine files (as we must to consolidate), we find thousands of hidden inconsistencies. One installation, for example, found 17 different techniques for storing part number. When they placed part number in a shared segment, they were forced to decide on a mutually agreeable format. By the same token, the same installation found that the part number was called by different names. And while it had the same meaning, it became known as the line item number for some, a part number for others, and catalog number for others. Realizing this, the installation assigned a unique name and format that had to be used by all personnel.

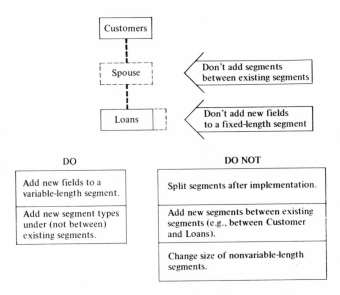

**Figure 4.39.** Do's and don'ts of evolutionary growth

By consolidating files, then, we've cleaned up the inconsistencies by generating *standard naming conventions and formats*. These conventions are then shared among application areas, making it easy for programmers to revise another person's code.

Since we're dealing with the same animal, we automatically become more familiar with his characteristics. In other words, programmers become more familiar with a "shared" data base than its file equivalent, which varies in design and format from one application to another. Familiarity with shared data bases results in faster revisions.

If we're using standard files, chances are that these files were originally created by an application program for a specific user. As time progresses, we tend to lose the relationship between File A/Program T23FILE and its user. By now, the jobs have been released to DP operations for production runs. It may possibly take DP operations several months to draw a schematic of files and application programs run daily, weekly, or monthly. In other words, it is hard to identify a file and its contents. Remember, medium-size installations average 300 to 500 unique files, each having its own format, naming conventions, etc.

Unlike the file environment, the data base environment has consolidated resources, making it easy to locate items within segments. First of all, the data bases are used by multiple application areas. Data base access would far exceed file access. Because of this, we have probably assigned data base design to one or more personnel members. The data base administrators (DBA) can provide application programmers with a description of each field within each segment. We therefore bypass the need to generate new files for new programmed services. The consolidation of information also allows the programmer to expedite coding.

Suppose the new programmed service requires some data that wasn't placed in the data base. Under these circumstances we have to evaluate the usage of these new items. If they are used frequently (e.g., daily), then we may want to place them in the data base. If they're monthly report-type items, we may choose to build a new file. In either case, we have a Data Base Administrator who can make the evaluation. This removes the responsibility from an unskilled employee (programmer) to a skilled employee (Data Base Administrator), who will access the situation with performance in mind.

Data base design, I'd like to add, should not be approached haphazardly. Unlike impulsive spending, data base design should be approached like a manager estimating his annual budget. We should choose one or more application areas, communicate with the end user and design for stability. Within one year's time, the original design and the resulting design should not change that much. We should revise the design as the company makes changes in its way of doing business or as we add new application areas. While the data base environment allows for more expedient changes, constant revisions allow for an unstable environment. Actually, this kind of instability reflects our approach to data base requirements.

In summary, data base evolution can be viewed as our ability to (1) add new application areas to an existing system, and (2) add new programmed services within a previously defined application. And while there are restrictions, we can minimize the impact of application program revisions by (1) defining variable length segments, (2) employing user-defined data independence, and (3) minimizing data base changes by carefully designing for each application. With this in mind, our cost savings areas are identifiable.

### Cost Savings Areas of Evolutionary Growth

Evolutionary growth provides the following advantages:

*New Applications (Functions):* We can share existing segments with new applications (e.g., customers being shared with checking account and personal loans).

We can append new fields to the end of a variable-length segment.

We can add new segment types without revising existing application programs.

*New Programmed Services for Existing Applications:* We can revise application programs with relative ease because we have standardized data elements.

We can add new application programs without adding new files (i.e., allow new programs to access existing segments).

We can add new segments for our new programmed services.

## Data Recovery

In today's world of data processing, we've all encountered the need for data recovery procedures, usually when we're exposed to our first emergency. I saw the need in January 1964 when I received a 3:00 A.M. telephone call for help. It seems that my files generated input/output errors on each attempt to execute. Without these "critical reports," of course, the company would be exposed to financial losses. What do we do when our files cannot be read? Well, 3:00 A.M. is not the best time for good, intelligent thinking.

Traditionally, we've approached error recovery by retaining several copies of the file (see Fig. 4.40).

In more recent years, of course, some installations have retained two copies of the most recent file (see Fig. 4.41). Nevertheless, our processing procedure retains its complexities.

Let's stop momentarily and review the need for file recovery procedures for non-DP veterans. When we automate an application, chances are that our volume of entries exceeds our card file facilities. To remove the need for card file backup, we created a second copy of the tape or disk file. We're protecting ourselves against the loss of a master file that cannot be recreated easily. We assume, and rightfully so, that if we encounter I/O errors on one file, there is a high probability that the second copy is readable.

File recovery procedures serve another function. As illustrated in Fig. 4.41,

**Figure 4.40.** Current approach to file recovery. The procedure dates back to the mid-sixties when EAM equipment was replaced by second-generation computers.

| Great-Grandfather (least recent) | Update Cards (12/15/69) | Grandfather (more recent) | Update Cards (12/22/69) | Father (current status) |

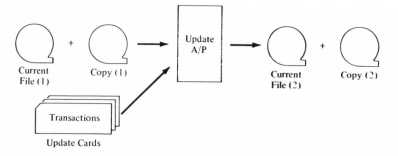

**Figure 4.41.** Retaining two copies of a current file at all times, the newer approach to data recovery

we need two copies of a file prior to update processing. Let's assume that the application program changes quantities. If it terminates abnormally (e.g., during the run), we will find it hard to locate the last updated record and continue updating from that point. Should this problem arise, we simply use the backup copy and start processing with transaction 1.

Now, while this is an excellent means of protecting our files, we've just increased our data processing requirements in several ways. First of all, we're using more CPU (central processing unit) time to copy tapes. Secondly, we're doubling operator efforts to mount and dismount devices, not to mention the clerical efforts required to manage our I/O devices. Thirdly, we're increasing our costs by a factor of 2 for I/O devices to store duplicate copies of critical files. And lastly, we're increasing our application program responsibilities to (1) document backup operating procedures, (2) assign initial devices and data set names, and (3) test these resources prior to releasing production jobs. (Remember that we're only discussing update processing.)

Good data base systems should provide users with "automatic" *data base recovery features* that reduce our current backup resources and procedures. I've used the word "features" because the software approach would perform several functions. Let's take them one at a time.

### Data Base Logging

Data base logging would entail copying the "changes" only. In other words, an application program would not update all record entries at any given time. If that is true, why copy all entries when only a small percentage has changed? Stated differently, a good data base system would "log" the before-and-after image of a "changed" segment regardless of the type of change (add, delete, or revise); see Fig. 4.42.

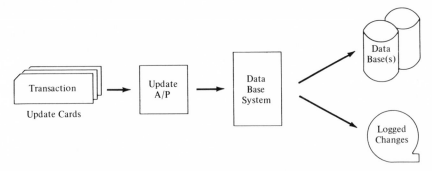

**Figure 4.42.** Using a data base system to log the "before" and "after" image of segment changes

Once the changes have been logged, we can then use the log tape if we encounter abnormal conditions. Let's review abnormal conditions and log recovery procedures.

### Data Base Backout

If we're in the process of updating a file when the application program terminates abnormally, we can use the log tape to back out changes so that we can reprocess the update program, as illustrated in Fig. 4.43.

### Data Base Recovery

Suppose we're attempting to process a retrieval program when we encounter I/O errors. In this case, we'd use the data base recovery feature (Fig. 4.44) to reconstruct the data base.

**Figure 4.43.** Using the data base system to back-out changes that were made prior to the abnormal termination

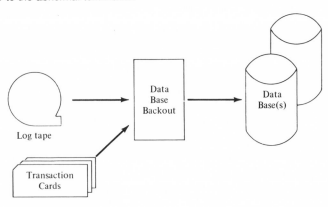

**Figure 4.44.** Using the data base system to recover (reconstruct) the data base if hardware I/O errors are detected

In essence, the data base recovery features remove these responsibilities from the application programmer. He need not document or test recovery procedures, since they have been placed in the data base system. Furthermore, we've reduced CPU utilization by logging only the "changed" segments. Now we can reduce I/O resources and operator services. These reductions are achieved by using the log tape accumulation feature, which is described next.

### Log Tape Accumulations

As update programs are executed, we start accumulating log tapes at the rate of one per update program execution. These log tapes can be merged into a single file (Fig. 4.45).

For those installations that retain two copies of each file, we could reduce their number of files (I/O devices) by 50%. In other words, these combined data base facilities eliminate the need to store duplicate copies of critical files.

There is one other factor of significance within the data base recovery feature. Some installations have large volumes of data residing on data bases. An insurance company, for example, used 30 IBM 3330 disk storage packs to store their customers. If we detect hardware I/O errors on one pack, do we have to "recover" the entire data base? Some data base systems allow the users to divide

**Figure 4.45.** Using a data base system to manage its own log tapes accumulated over time

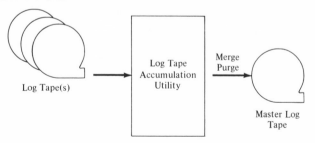

the data base into several data sets. In this way, data base recovery is on the data set level as opposed to the data base level. The insurance company, for example, could divide its data base into ten data sets (three 3330's per data set). Data base recovery would then recover three 3330's instead of thirty 3330's, thereby reducing recovery time.

I've used the words "automatic" data base recovery, a term that deserves clarification. While data base systems have "coded" services for logging, backout, log accumulation, and recovery, these have to be "triggered" by the operator. The "triggering" procedure, however, can be defined by the Data Base Administrator for all installation data bases. Once they have been defined, these steps can be submitted to DP operations for production services. Here again we're consolidating resources and operating procedures for the entire installation.

In conclusion, data base recovery has a significant impact on our operating procedures. The following cost savings can be derived.

### Cost-Savings in Data Base Recovery

Data base recovery derives the following advantages:

*File (I/O Device) Reduction:* By logging update changes, we reduce the need to store backup copies of master files.

*CPU Usage Reduction:* By logging changes only, we reduce the number of I/O activities otherwise required to "copy" the entire file.

By backing-out changes, we reduce I/O activities otherwise required to reproduce the file.

*Operator Intervention Reduction:* By having these services within the data base system, we reduce device mounting and operator procedures for each application program.

*Programmer Responsibility Reductions:* By having these services within the data base system, we eliminate the need to test and document recovery procedures for each application program.

## Programmer Productivity

We use the words "programmer productivity" as a catchall phrase to examine programmer responsibilities and means of improving his resources. From this, we hope to increase programmer productivity.

In the traditional approach to data processing, application programmers perform any tasks external to coding programmed services. These tasks range from file design to operating procedures of a new program. While programmer tasks vary (in the name of progress), we continue to emphasize "coding" in their planned education.

Within the past five years, we've started teaching programmers to "debug" their code. I've often wondered if many of the poorly written, poorly documented programs that have accumulated over the years didn't stem from tying the programmer's hands behind his back while asking him why the deadline hasn't been met. Now let's define the education curriculum in a standard application programmer's environment and equate it to the real world.

### Education Curriculum for Application Programmers

The units of the education curriculum are as follows:

*Programming Language*
Teach student to define an application using a programming language.

*Programming Techniques*
Teach student to approach an application with performance techniques in mind. Code efficiency is emphasized.

*File Design*
Teach student file design and access techniques, using their programming language. File recovery should be emphasized.

*Machine Operations*
Teach student basic principles of computer and operating systems, job entry preparation and submission.

*Documentation Procedures*
Teach student documentation standards, including device allocation, naming conventions, and other installation procedures.

*Debugging Techniques*
Teach student coding techniques that aid him during application program testing. Should abnormal termination occur, teach student to read computer dumps and locate source of problem.

Most installations have not trained their programmers adequately. Most programmers have attended a programming course only. This education gap leaves room for many assumptions and hidden problems that are undetected before the programs are ultimately run. Coding efficiency, storage estimates, and performance considerations aren't really considered until we have encountered operating problems. In truth, the need to "clean up" our application programs may be long overdue.

Again, migration toward a data base system gives us an excellent opportunity to "clean house" in this area. We could discard dead programs (those that run but aren't really used), define today's user requirements, and enhance programmer efficiency simultaneously. Let's take these one at a time by first relating improved programming techniques to the data base features previously discussed.

With *file consolidation,* we will be assigning data base design to a Data Base Administrator. He will be responsible for design, access, and maintenance of installation data bases. By doing so, we're removing file design, device allocation, and maintenance from *each* application programmer.

With file consolidation, we're also centralizing the processed items. Instead of sort routines, multiple file access, and search routines, the application references a shared data base. We can remove the input/output code that resides within the application program. By doing so, we reduce coding, testing, and debugging of standard I/O operations.

With *data independence,* we can permit an application program to access a "subset" of the total structure. By doing so, we define only those segments that are required for processing. In other words, the application programmer need not be familiar with nonprocessed segments. His segment descriptions would therefore be smaller than the description of multiple files. Essentially, application programming for segment descriptions should be less than field descriptions for multiple files.

With data independence of data base attributes, we're stabilizing application programs while varying our resources to meet changing times. Unlike files, we can change devices (from sequential to random access, etc.) or change other physical characteristics without changing application programs. This enhancement has a tremendous but subtle impact on our data processing performance. For the first time, we can vary our hardware I/O resources without revising our application programs. This prevents our hardware from becoming obsolete in lieu of program revisions.

With *evolutionary growth* we again leave room for changing our data base scope without application program revisions. We can add new application areas and new segments to our system without impacting our current users. This assumes, of course, that new areas do not cause a change in segment relationships.

With *data base recovery,* we are automating file recovery procedures. This removes file maintenance and backup procedures from the list of procedures currently assigned to application programmers.

Let's summarize the above enhancements in this manner. Chances are that we assume a lot from our programmers. Chances are that all of our "assumptions" aren't expressed and those that are—well, we leave it to the programmer's incentive to get the job done. This results in learning things the hard way, that is, by applying elementary techniques to advanced applications. By letting each programmer ''do his own thing,'' we end up with essentially that—''things.''

I'd love to tell you a few war stories about European trips and cross-country flights to fix emergencies that took half a day to repair. The errors were generated from ''assuming'' things I'd think belonged in a beginner programming class. But while these stories would humor you, I'm afraid they're a little frightening when we ask, ''What's going on in my shop?''

The point is this: We have more problems than will ever meet our conscious minds. We simply compensate them with virtual memory, larger computing systems, and improved hardware gear. Good data base systems can force us to clean house in file design and application programming. These systems have many programmer productivity aids, the best one being the removal of responsibilities that programmers haven't been trained to handle. A typical clean-up of file design and application programming is illustrated in Fig. 4.46.

Now that we've covered programmer productivity relative to the data base features already discussed, let's look at some additional productivity aids that relate directly to coding.

With traditional files, programmers have to define all the fields in their application programs. If they want to compare fields, they have to read each record, compare the fields, and match the search criteria so that they can process

**Figure 4.46.** Removing responsibilities from application programmers. The result: code and document programs.

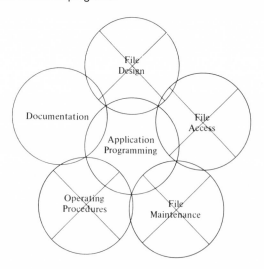

the record. Now all these decisions are coded into the application program. Since each programmer codes differently, the amount of code, coding efficiency, test time, etc., will vary among programmers.

Some data base systems will search record (segment) entries if the application program passes the search criteria to them. The delinquent payment program, for example, may want to locate any loans for which payments haven't been received. Instead of searching each payments segment, the application program could request the following:

| PAYMENTS | (DATE | > 01/15/75) |
|----------|-------|-------------|
| ↓ | ↓ | ↓ |
| Segment | Field | Sought |
| Type | (data element) | Value |

The data base system interprets this as follows:

LOOK AT THE PAYMENTS segment
LOOK FOR THE DATE FIELD
IF THE DATE IS GREATER THAN 01/15/75, RETURN IT TO ME.

The data base system then searches for a payments segment that qualifies and returns it to the application program. By doing so, we're reducing program code, variations in coding techniques, and test time for application programs. I have seen an application program written and tested within two weeks at one installation. I was astounded because I'd seen the same installation site six-month estimates to write an application in the file environment.

Now that we've discussed the removal of file search routines, let's look at the removal of sort routines. A file can be sorted in only one major sequence. That is, the checking account file can be sorted by customer name or account number, but not both simultaneously. As a result, files are sorted for one sequence and then another. Some data base systems have removed the need to sort by using a feature called "secondary indexing." (While this is a powerful data base feature, I've included it here because it improves programmer productivity.)

*Secondary indexing* is a means by which we can store alternate indexes that provide "automatic sort" capabilities. The customer data base, for example, may be sorted by customer name. Suppose we have the need to sort these segments by account number. Instead of sorting segments, we can build an alternate search capability for the data base.

Stated differently, secondary indexing is analogous to the card catalog found in libraries. We physically store the books by topic. We then build catalogs to

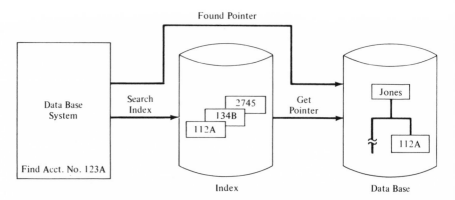

**Figure 4.47.** Using Secondary Indexing to locate segments that are stored in a different sort sequence

reference (index) the books by author, title, and subject. To locate a book by a particular author, we search the author catalog. This eliminates the need to search all books within that topic, or to re-sort all books within that topic.

Secondary indexes work in the same manner. We can reference the secondary index (catalog) to locate the account number. We can then access the data base, going directly to the customer who has that account number (see Fig. 4.47). We could extend this feature by adding more search fields to the secondary index. Suppose, for example, we wanted to distinguish between car loans and boat loans. We could append the account number to the loan type (Fig. 4.48).

To use these indexes, the application program issues the same request shown earlier. It need not distinguish between segment fields and secondary index fields. This becomes the responsibility of the data base system.

The best features of secondary indexing include: data independence (application programs need not know their physical characteristics) and index maintenance (when updates occur on the indexed field(s), these changes are made to the secondary index data base(s). With secondary indexing we also have ''true'' evolutionary growth. We can add new secondary indexes without impacting application programs that do not need the alternate search capability. Thus, we can reference segments in different sort sequences without changing (sorting) the physical data or changing application programs.

Secondary indexing should be defined by the Data Base Administrator, who is responsible for defining all data base resources. By doing so, we are removing another responsibility from *each application programmer*. (This removal of responsibility also falls into the category of untrained programmer skills.)

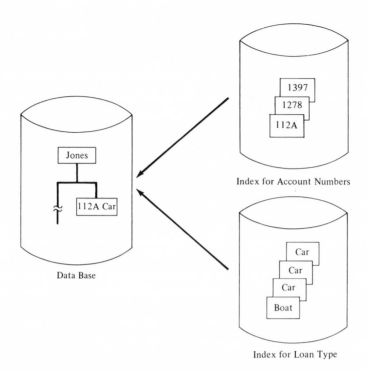

**Figure 4.48.** Using Secondary Indexes to sort keys and their qualifiers. Programs can search for Account Number or Loan Type, using this secondary index.

The last feature we'll discuss is *logical relationships*. Logical relationship is a means by which programmers can "automatically" cross-reference data bases. Let's assume, for example, that a production site created a parts master data base (Fig. 4.49). Now suppose we placed a purchase order for parts when their inventory status indicated a shortage. The probability is that we'd want to know the quantity on order and the promised delivery date. We could store this in a new segment type, called "orders" (Fig. 4.50).

Assume that we had automated the purchase order system. The orders information already exists in our purchase order data base (Fig. 4.51). Should we allow the application program to access both data bases or should we store duplicate orders information in our parts master data base? If we carry duplicate orders segments, who will maintain the status in both data bases?

Instead of duplicating segment type and duplicating segment maintenance, we could employ *logical* relationships. In this way, we let the data base system access and maintain our segments. To do this, we define a processing relationship between both data bases (see Fig. 4.52).

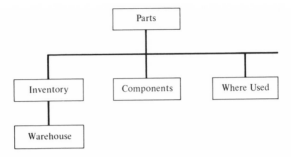

**Figure 4.49.** Using a Parts Master Data Base to identify production parts, their components and usage and the inventory status

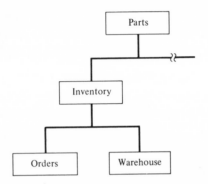

**Figure 4.50.** Adding the Orders segment to trace parts on order and their promised shipment date

**Figure 4.51.** Deciding how to access data. Let application program reference both data bases or duplicate segment in Parts Master Data Base.

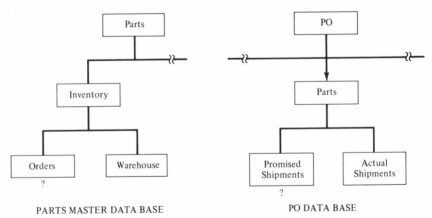

PARTS MASTER DATA BASE                    PO DATA BASE

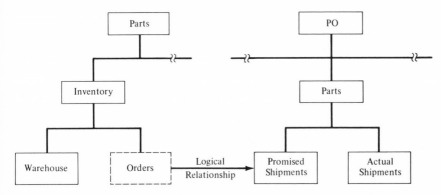

**Figure 4.52.** Using Logical Relationships to access one or more data bases "automatically." That is, the data base system will reference both data bases for the application program.

In the preceding example, the application program can request the orders segment. This unreal (virtual) segment causes the data base system to enter the purchase order data base and return "prom shipments" (promised shipments) data to the program. The application programmer need not know that two data bases are physically accessed or maintained by the data base system.

*Logical relationship* is another powerful tool, allowing installations to relate data bases in many varying ways. With maximum usage of this feature, we could develop a network of interrelated data base structures. By combining secondary indexing with logical relationships, we could probably define all of our processing requirements with a minimum number of physical data bases. This could be achieved with relative ease because we are finally removing nonprogramming responsibilities from the application programmer.

In summary, good data base systems provide for a consolidation of resources throughout the installation. These resources include both manpower and machines. The application programmer, in particular, inherits numerous programming aids that let him concentrate on coding. These aids are listed below.

### Programmer Productivity Aids

Consolidation of resources provides a number of aids to the application programmer, as follows:

1. *File Consolidation:* By merging interrelated files into a "shared" data base, the application can access centralized (nonfragmented) resources with relative ease.

2. *Data Independence:* By "system" access of requested segments, we reduce the amount of coding and access of segments that are not processed by an application program.

By "system" access of physical devices (I/O activities), we can vary our hardware gear without changing our application programs.

By system access of secondary indexes, we can access segments in different sort sequences without changing application programs or physically sorting our data.

By system access of logical relationships, we can merge data bases into a network-type system without duplicating segments, maintaining duplicate segments—or defining the entire data base capability to any one application programmer.

3. *Evolutionary Growth:* By adding new segment types (that don't change the relationship of existing segments), we can add new application areas without changing existing application programs.

By adding new secondary indexes, we can change our access sequence without physically changing the data or existing application programs.

4. *Data Recovery:* By receiving "automatic" data base management and maintenance, we remove file recovery from the application programmer.

5. *Reduction in Coding:* Having removed total file (data base) definition and sort routines, we've reduced application coding.

By using system request techniques, we've removed the need for record search routines.

# 5 Highlights of the Data Base Era

The real significance of the data base era does not reside in program product features, for they are only the means to an end. The real significance of the data base era resides in the implementation of the features described in this publication. That is, we can use file consolidation to design integrated systems, and use data independence to add new data processing requirements with relative ease and data recovery to automate fileback procedures. To examine these enhancements, let's review the types of data processing systems that are usually installed at most installations (see Fig. 5.1).

## Types of Data Processing Systems

Based on the complexity of each system, we are often forced to design it as a separate entity of the corporation. That is, the production control system will be installed and after its completion the purchasing system can be installed. When the purchasing system is complete, we can proceed to install the accounts payable system. Oftentimes, as we implement new systems, we discover that a large percentage of the data element requirements exists in other systems. However, file-dependent code prevents us from revising the file design in order to stabilize the existing system(s) application programs. And so we find ourselves creating new files for new systems, and sometimes we find ourselves creating interface files between systems (Fig. 5.2).

Having been restricted by file-dependent code, we probably would find an 85% overhead of redundant (repetitious) data among files belonging to different data processing systems. And with redundant data comes the need for duplicate update processing to synchronize the status of the same information, and duplicate update application programs and duplicate backup files (and their backup

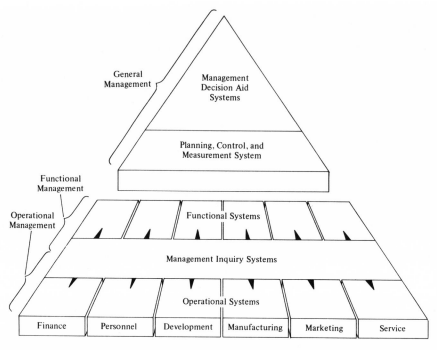

**Figure 5.1.** Our approach to implementation begins with the operational systems that service specific application areas.

**Figure 5.2.** Using interface files to update the same information in another data processing system

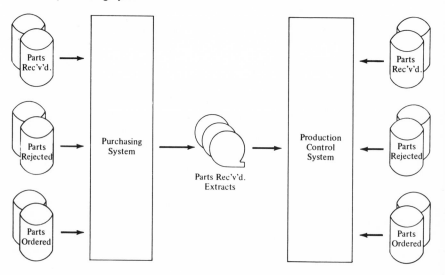

procedures). With good data base systems (that contain most, if not all, of the features described within this publication), we can consolidate the files and reduce our data processing overhead. To do this, we start with a single data processing system and examine its files. In the purchasing system, for example, one installation installed 551 files, in which 117 files contained the part number. If we were to place part number information in a data base system that supports hierarchical structuring, we could consolidate the 117 files, as shown in Fig. 5.3.

To consolidate a given application area, we have to analyze its files in order to design a hierarchically structured data base. This process is the inverse of systems design as we are accustomed to doing. During systems design and analysis, we examine the total data processing requirements and divide those requirements into subsets. Each subset is analyzed for detail data processing requirements in which we derive (1) data element requirements, and (2) application program specifications. From this point forward, our files are designed and our application programs are tested during the implementation phase.

With data base design, we are starting with an existing system * and analyz-

---

* If we are implementing a new system, we will perform the same implementation steps as standard file design. Instead of creating files, we will use our file design requirements as input to data base design and implementation.

**Figure 5.3.** Replacing the 117 files with a hierarchically structured Parts Master Data Base

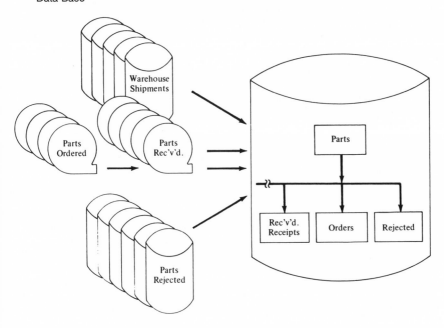

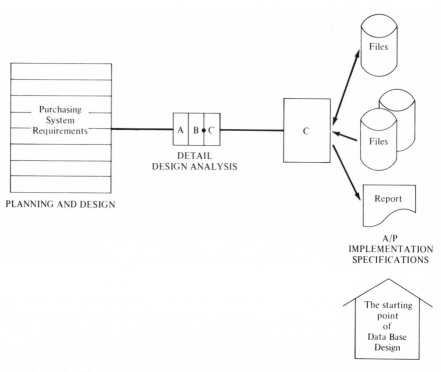

**Figure 5.4.** The starting point of data base design when we are consolidating files from existing systems

ing the data elements that have already been placed on files. In other words, we start at the detail level of an existing system, examining files 001 through 117 in order to design the segment types within the data base (Fig. 5.4).

In a data base environment, then, we will be consolidating files and integrating systems that are interrelated. And with this approach comes the need for new areas of specialization. Since our files are being consolidated, we need personnel responsible for consolidating our files and designing data base segments.

## Data Base Administration

As shown in Fig. 5.5, we've created a new area of specialization, called data base administration. Within this function, we have design, implementation, and maintenance responsibilities. Let's explore these functions further. To design a data base, the Data Base Administrator needs processing statistics, such as:

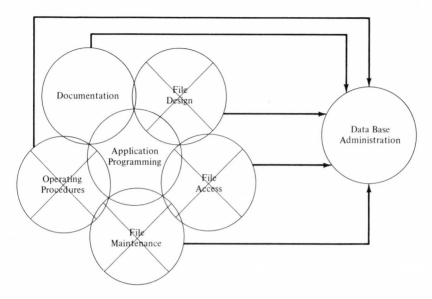

**Figure 5.5.** Reassigning file-oriented responsibilities to Data Base Administration

File contents
    Field contents
    Field format
    Field usage
        Update type (delete, add, replace)
        Update frequency
        Retrieval frequency
    Field retention span

Most important is that the Administrator needs to know the frequency of access and the type of access. This is analogous to daily filing. We would not want the most frequently accessed items to be hard to locate in our closets.

The Data Base Administrator therefore designs for performance, using statistics to compute anticipated traffic volume (see Fig. 5.6). Once he has received processing volumes and their frequency, he can merge files into a "shared" data base. After designing the data base, he can document its contents. Since he knows "shared" and "mutually exclusive" segments, he then distributes the segment descriptions to application analysts. The analysts receive descriptions of "shared" segments and their application's segment types. In other words,

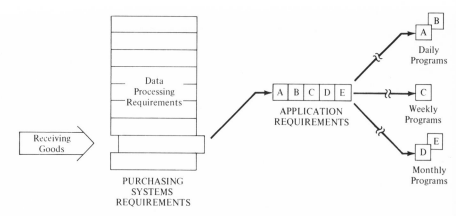

**Figure 5.6.** Using the processing frequency to employ data base design techniques that would improve performance

analysts in the Payroll Department do not receive a description of parts segments belonging to the Manufacturing Department.

Once data base design and documentation have been completed, the Data Base Administrator *defines* the design(s) to the data base system. This requires special system coding that results in control blocks and tables that are accessed by the data base system.

At this point, the Data Base Administrator can assign I/O devices and generate the necessary control information required for program access and data base

**Figure 5.7.** A *functional* diagram of responsibilities as they flow from one area of specialization to another

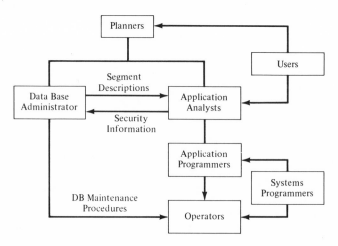

maintenance. Sometimes, installations create test data bases whereby application programmers test their code. If this is the case, data base administrators can test system maintenance utilities and document maintenance procedures for DP operations. Otherwise, these utilities have to be tested with production data bases.

As application programs are written, the analyst passes program names and "authorized" segment names to the Data Base Administrator. He then codes their security control blocks and builds these members for systems access.

Should problems arise with production *data bases,* these problems are taken to the Data Base Administrator. Thus, he becomes responsible for designing, revising, and reorganizing data bases and maintaining log tapes. He is also responsible for monitoring data base usage and performance.

The Data Base Administrator is our only new area of specialization in the data base environment. The other areas (Fig. 5.7) of specialization remain intact.

# Educational Criteria in Areas of Specialization

All of these areas of specialization need training in the data base system you've chosen. Let's review the education criteria for each area of specialization (refer to Fig. 5.8). (We're assuming that most customers want all the features previously discussed. Otherwise, we have overdefined education.)

*Planners:* Responsible for overall plan and control of design, implementation, and future enhancements. Plan and monitor hardware, software and implementation procedures.

Courses would include (1) Introduction, (2) Concepts and Facilities, and (3) Implementation Guidelines

(Some installations allow planners to select software packages, while others rely on corporate decisions to set the trend for growth and change. If planners select software, they need courses that describe several software packages.)

*Data Base Administrator:* Designs, implements, and maintains the data base systems where maintenance includes data base recovery and performance.

Courses would include (1) Introduction, (2) Concepts and Facilities, (3) Data Base Design and Implementation, and (4) Security Procedures and Guidelines.

*Application Analyst:* Communicates with users and converts their processing requirements into program specifications. Converses with Data Base

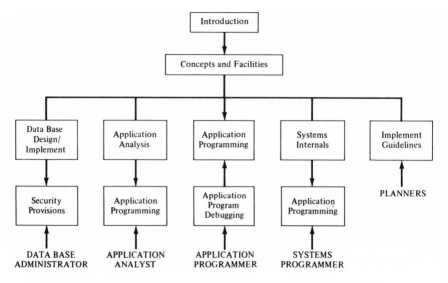

**Figure 5.8.** Education guidelines for each area of specialization in a data base environment

Administrator on processing requirements and processing frequency. Helps define security control blocks for each application program.

Courses would include (1) Introduction, (2) Concepts and Facilities, (3) Application Analysis of Data Base systems, and (4) Application Programming.

*Application Programmer:* Designs and codes application programs for the data base system. Tests, debugs, and documents program. Communicates with users on processed service results. Converses with systems programmer with debugging aid.

Courses would include (1) Introduction, (2) Concepts and Facilities, and (3) Application Programming.

*Systems Programmer:* Generates SYSGEN (*System Gen*eration) data base system. Maintains current release and helps programmers debut problems.

Courses would include (1) Introduction, (2) Concepts and Facilities, (3) Application Programming, and (4) Systems Internal Logic.

*Users:* Define processing requirements and processing frequency (daily, weekly, monthly; and volume of transactions).\*

---

\* Although users are not within the Data Processing Organization, you will want to give them a seminar to acquaint them with your new data base System.

A course would include an in-house seminar on the benefits of the system, and the need for joint efforts. Should stimulate and stress the need to examine reports and their "real value."

I've included application programming in several areas of specialization, such as in application analysis, application programming, and systems programming. This is required because areas of specialization create dependency on "group efforts." Like the medical profession, we need a basis for understanding areas that overlap. Otherwise, we leave room for confusion. Unlike the medical profession, our specialized areas interact daily, not as an emergency warrants. Since an analyst designs programs and supervises their completion, he should know coding techniques. Because systems programmers help application programmers debug problems, they should be able to read core dumps and programmer code. These three areas overlap in this respect, as illustrated in Fig. 5.9.

Another interdependent area of specialization lies in data base design. Some installations recommend that application analysts design the program's segments, using frequency and volume statistics. If this is done, we need to train the application analyst in data base design considerations. This would certainly help the Data Base Administrator (especially with communication), but its overall usefulness should depend upon the number and complexity of your data base resources.

Having discussed education requirements in the data base era, let's just summarize by saying that data base education is better than its predecessors in other areas. We are beginning to recognize the need to tailor education to job responsibilities. This has resulted in course development that is aimed at a specific audience (or specialized functions). Today, we can find courses for application programmers *or* application analysts, etc. This mode of education reduces the probability of "assumed" knowledge instead of "assumed" responsibilities.

At the present time, however, we haven't defined curricula whereby each

**Figure 5.9.** Interdependent functions being performed by three different areas of specialization

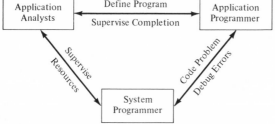

course prepares a student for a more advanced course (e.g. introductory, intermediate, and advanced). This form of education would greatly improve productivity because it allows the student to build up his expertise. That is, he can learn A and use it prior to being exposed to A' in a classroom or working environment. And being exposed in a working environment *first* may be the source of many hidden system degradations.

And, finally, we need to emphasize education curricula that interrelate areas of specialization (Fig. 5.10). In other words, where do functions begin and end? If the application analyst provides program specifications to the application programmers, what should be in the specifications? If resources are missing, where should the information be found? Actually, we can compare the DP environment with the medical profession. We know that dentists specialize in teeth, pediatricians in childhood diseases, and allergists in allergies. Yet these specialized areas relate directly to child-care services. Data processing requirements function in the same manner. All of our resources are geared to providing computing services; we should be able to draw a fine line between various personnel responsibilities required to transfer program phases from one function to another.

For information to flow smoothly between functions, we need to treat program service requests as if they were products being manufactured. Thus, we know that a product starts with specifications (e.g., user requirements). To manufacture the product, we need to analyze product specifications to establish feasibility (e.g., systems analysis). Once the product has been approved for manufacture, we document manufacturing procedures for using raw materials (e.g., application analysis). These procedures are passed to our plant for implementation (e.g., application programming). Our plant uses product control to test the

**Figure 5.10.** The flow of programmed services beginning with requirements and ending with test and debug procedures

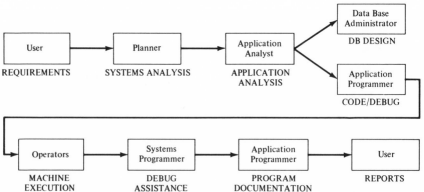

quality of our finished product (e.g., test and debug, using operators and systems programmers). Upon completion of this procedure, we have a finished product (e.g., production programs).

As I've indicated above, our application programs go through a similar procedure. And while we've identified the functions, we haven't developed procedures to carry the product from one function to another. To start doing so, we first need to teach personnel the "common" elements of data processing. This is equivalent to the medical profession in that employees would have a "common" understanding of the profession. For this reason, I have placed Introduction and Concepts and Facilities in each specialized area listed previously as an education criterion.

In addition to training, we need to define the "fine line" between functions. Let's start examining the functions in a file environment by posing a few pertinent questions:

*What process is completed in each function? What functions should be merged together? For example, does application analysis and application programming = program analysts?*

*What forms should be designed within each function?*

*What forms would help the product to flow smoothly from one function to another?*

In truth, we need to treat data processing services as though they were manufactured products, with the same smooth flow from one stage of production to another. Without it, we are haphazardly approaching data processing.

The data base environment is similar to the file environment in that the functions remain intact. We should have fewer problems because good data base systems have automated some of our manual chores. For a Data Base Administrator, we've also centralized file design/maintenance chores. Yet, the need for function definition and form remains there. We are still working with a product that passes through different functions. The need for "process control" gives us a smoother operating environment with "trace" capability. That is, we can trace the stages and estimate our time more wisely.

When training your staff for a new data base system, allocate time for trial and error. In other words, train your staff for six months prior to exposing them to your requirements. Some data base systems distribute test systems with their package. Using their test environment, you could let the staff test and debug application problems on a half-time basis. That way, you're building up their expertise as opposed to experiencing the results of the learning curve in production jobs. Six months at half-time assignments may seem long, but let's view time realistically. What is the difference between a six-month delay in a good system and the infinite life cycle of a bad system? At this point, we may relate the latter case to three prominent DP quotes:

"You get what you pay for."

"Garbage in—garbage out."
(GIGO, my first DP training.)

"We can always afford to do it over later, but can never afford to do it right initially."

Now, with trained personnel (and with the new specialized areas of data base administration), let's proceed to consolidate our files for a given application area (refer to Fig. 5.11). To do this, we examine each data element and its relationship to other data elements for each file within a subset (such as parts received) and build the segments as described in storage reduction (Chapter 4). The end result will be one of sharing commonly used data among subsets within a given application area, as shown in Fig. 5.11.

**Figure 5.11.** Using a hierarchical structure to consolidate files within a given application area

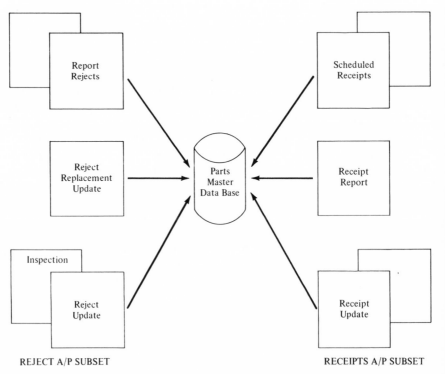

REJECT A/P SUBSET                RECEIPTS A/P SUBSET

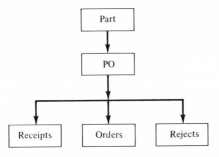

**Figure 5.12.** File consolidation by sharing part information with all the application programs that need to access that information

If we have used the design techniques that were described in the section "File Consolidation" (Chapter 4), our data base design for part information within the purchasing system should appear as shown in Fig. 5.12. In other words, the part segment contains all the data elements required to describe a given part; the PO segment contains all the data elements required to describe a purchase order for a given part; and receipts segments contain the data elements required to monitor the receipt status for a given PO order, etc. The overall enhancements include (1) file reduction, because we have a centralized source of information; (2) update processing reduction, because one update makes the most recent information available to all the application programs; (3) update program reduction, because one update program is revising a segment for all the applications within purchasing; and (4) backup file reduction, because we have fewer files to protect.

Once we have completed design requirements (and implementation) for a given system, we can proceed to analyze and implement other systems within the installation. And with each new system implementation, our data base design will be revised to include new data element requirements. Suppose, for example, we implemented all the systems within operations. What would be in our parts master data base upon completion? To answer this, let's examine the functional flow of information within a corporation (see Fig. 5.13).

## The Functional Flow of Information

We approach our analysis of corporate information flow by defining the more common accounts and departments, and their functions.

*Order Entry:* A request for a specific product triggers an order to Inventory Control. (Billing retains copy and awaits manufacturing before billing customer.)

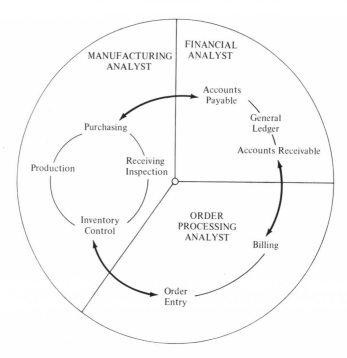

**Figure 5.13.** The functional flow of information as it is processed by different application areas within the corporation

*Inventory Control:* Since a product is composed of raw materials (parts), this department uses the inventory status of parts to trigger a request to Production Control.

*Production Control:* This department (1) schedules production; (2) revises the inventory status, and (3) (if necessary) releases a parts requisition to Purchasing.

*Purchasing:* This department (1) issues a purchase order; (2) notifies the receiving dock of promised deliveries; (3) notifies Quality Assurance if parts are to be inspected; and (4) notifies the vendor when parts are rejected. For satisfactory orders, Purchasing notifies Accounts Payable to pay vendors.

*Accounts Payable:* Using the Purchasing Department information, this department pays the vendor and charges the amount paid against Production.

*General Ledger:* Using the various department charges, production costs, and customer orders, this department balances cost against expenses to determine profit.

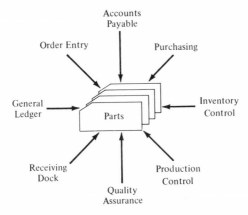

**Figure 5.14.** The functional flow of part information within a corporation

*Accounts Receivable:* Upon completion of manufacturing, testing, and shipping, the customer is billed for the product. This department bills and monitors collection of dollars.

Now let's isolate part information and examine the applications areas that process information on part status (see Fig. 5.14).

If we employed data base design for all the application areas within a given corporation, our resultant data base design would appear as in Fig. 5.15.

In Fig. 5.15, parts and inspection segments would be processed by applica-

**Figure 5.15.** Merging the data element requirements for part information into a shared data base

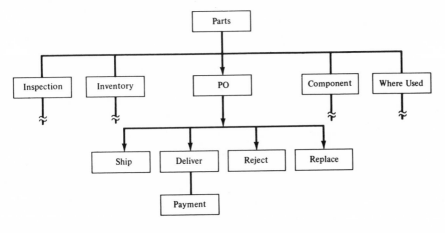

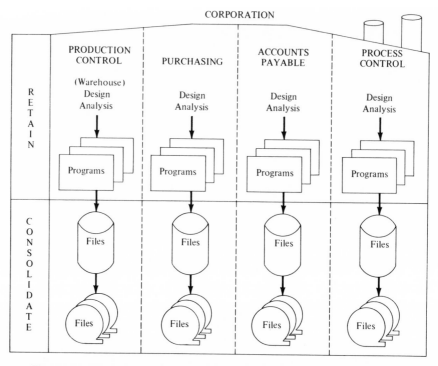

**Figure 5.16.** Through hierarchical data base design files can be consolidated while retaining specific application program functions.

**Figure 5.17.** Retaining a minimum set of data while maximizing its functional usage through application programs

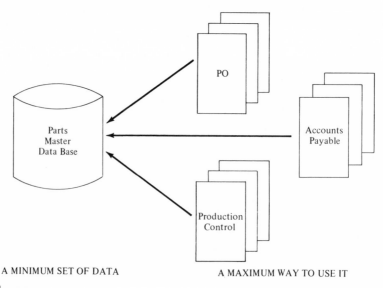

104

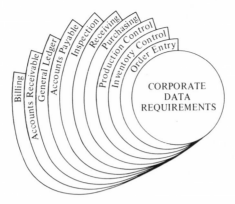

**Figure 5.18.** Hierarchically structured data base design allows definition of a minimum set of corporate data—regardless of its usage in application areas.

tion programs written for Quality Assurance, while parts, components, and where-used segments would be processed by application programs written for Production Control. The remaining segment types would be processed by application programs written for Purchasing and Accounts Payable departments. In essence, we would be consolidating information used commonly by application areas within the corporation (see Fig. 5.16), and the difference in functional area usage would occur through application programs (Fig. 5.17). The parts receipt application would process its segment types and perform the same processed results for Production Control as occurred in a file design environment.

In essence, we are performing the same programmed services from a shared data base, as opposed to files, in a hierarchical structure (Fig. 5.18) that defines a minimum set of corporate data. Thus, the data base era should represent a new way of data management, and the new way should offer enhancements over standard file design. And the real enhancements should result in storing a minimum set of data elements within corporations. By doing so, we reduce a number of data processing resources while improving the integrity of reported information among application areas.

## A Point of Clarification

There have been some questions raised on the term "planner." The planner is a person who outlines the total system and divides its requirements into manageable subsets for application analysts. In some installations, this functional responsibility is performed by employees with varying titles (such as Lead Programmer, Programmer Analyst, Systems Designer), depending upon the size of a data processing installation and the scope of systems implementation. Far be it from me to say which title best describes the functional responsibilities of planning for the design of a system.

Within this publication, I have used the word "planner" to describe the functional responsibilities required to design a medium-to-large scale system, such as Purchasing or Production Control. The planner has been given the overall responsibility for defining the subsets of a given system (such as PO orders; parts receipts, etc.), documenting each subset for application analysts, and monitoring each stage of implementation. In other words, he has the overall responsibility for the system—from the time it is approved until its completion. And while this is not a new area of specialization, it may warrant clarification for readers familiar with other job titles.

# Index

Access 43-44, 73
Accounting machines 17, 18
Accounts payable 102
Accounts receivable 103
Adding to existing systems and application
    areas 26-39
Administration, Data base 92-95
Analysts: *see* Application analysts
Application analysts 5, 6, 7, 95-96
Application program(mer)s 19-21, 104
   addition to existing area 26-36
   education 80-87, 96
   multiple 3-4
   problems 44
   reduction 12

Backing-out changes 79
Backout, Data base 77
Backup 54
   files 8
   reduction 101

Cards, Punched 19
Changes, Data base 64
Clerical reduction 12, 58
Codes
   file-dependent 39
   format type 29
Coding, Reduction in 88
Common data base 52, 56
Compilers 3
Computer performance (improvement) 64

Consolidation
   files 2, 14, 48-58, 73, 81, 87, 92
   program 69
Contents, File 42
Control systems, Corporate analysis of 8-16
Cost savings
   computer performance 62
   data base recovery 79
   data independence 64
   evolutionary growth areas 74-75
   file consolidation 58
   storage reduction 48
Costs 44
CPU usage reduction 79
Customer/application relationship 44

Data
   duplicate or redundant 8, 9, 40, 41, 89
   element 21
   independence 58-64, 81, 88
   integrity 56, 58
   management problems 42-44
   processing systems 89-92
   recovery 75-79, 81, 88
   set 21
Data base
   administration 92-95
   backout 77
   changes 64
   defined 13, 52
   design 74, 91, 92, 94, 97, 103
   environment 10, 11, 12, 15-16

Data base (*continued*)
  logging 76-77
  security 64-69
Data base systems 11, 14, 94
  defined 13
  objectives 10
  *see also* Good data base system
Debugging 80
Delayed reactions 44
Design
  application program 44
  modifications 42
  *see also* Files (design)
Designers: *see* Systems (designers)
Documentation 80
Duplication 8, 9, 14, 40, 41, 89

Education 80-87, 95-101
Evolutionary growth 69-75, 81, 88
Excessive input/output operations 35
Excessive resources 15

Field-level security 68
Field/data set 17-18
File-dependent code 39, 89
Files 42-44
  backup 8
  consolidation 2, 14, 48-58, 73, 81, 87,
    92
  defined 21
  design 22-26, 36, 80
  interface 89, 91
  problems in processing 40
  reduction 79, 101
  standard 73
Fixed-length record format 22, 30, 33, 36,
  46
Format
  change 31
  fixed-length record 22, 30, 33, 36, 46
  type codes 29
  undefined record 25-26
  variable-length record 23-25
  *see also* Files (design)

General ledger 102
General-purpose systems 3

Good data base system 45, 62, 87, 91
Growth, Evolutionary 69-75, 81, 88

Hierarchical structure 46-47, 51-53, 58,
  100, 105

Implementing new system 37-38
Implementation
  bottlenecks 2, 14-15
  process 5
Indexing, Secondary 83-84
Information, Functional flow of 101-105
Input/output channels 3
Input-output operations, Excessive 35
Interface files 89, 91
Interpreters 17, 18
Inventory control 102

Keypunch 18

Log tape accumulations 78-79
Logging
  changes 79
  data base 76-77
Logical relationships 85, 87

Machine operations 80
Maintenance
  application program 44
  file 43
Multiple application programs 3-4
Multiple file access 43-44

Operating system 35
  extensions 4-16
Operator intervention reduction 79
Order entry 101

Planners 95, 106
Problems
  data management 42-44
  file processing 40
Process control 99
Production control 102
Production data bases 95
Programmer
  productivity 79-88

responsibility reduction 79
 systems 96
Program(mer)s, Application: *see* Application program(mer)s
Programming
 flexibility 64
 language and techniques 80
Programs
 consolidation 69
 logic reduction 58
 multiple application 3-4
 update 8
Punched cards 19
Purchasing 102

Record 21
Recovery
 data 75-79
 procedures (file) 43
Reduction 12, 58, 79, 101
 coding 88
Redundant data: *see* Duplication
Report contents 44
Reproducers 17, 18

Secondary indexing 83-84
Security
 data base 64-69
 field level 68
 segment level 65-67
Segment growth potential 64

Segment level 59
 control 69
 security 65
Shared data base 55-56, 58, 72, 73, 93
Shared segments 68, 71
Single data processing system 91
Single file access 43
Software support 3
Sorters 17, 18
Standard files 11, 73
Storage
 devices 42
 reduction 12, 46-48, 58
Systems
 designers 5
 general-purpose 3
 operating 14, 15, 35
 programmers 96

Terminology (new) 1
Test data bases 95
Test systems 99
Triggering procedure 79

Undefined record format 25-26
Update processing (and program reduction) 101
Updating 56-58
 programs 8

Variable-length record format 23-25
Variable-length segments 60, 61, 70-72, 74

Randall Library – UNCW

QA76.9.D3 P78                                          NXWW
Prothro / Information management systems : data ba

304900229154$